COMPLETE

STEM SMART

SCIENCE TECHNOLOGY ENGINEERING MATH

Grade 4

ISBN: 978-1-77149-508-0

Printed in China

Dear Parents and Guardians,

The acronym "**STEM**" stands for "**S**cience, **T**echnology, **E**ngineering, and **M**ath." These four fields of integrated study are essential to children in developing problem-solving and analytical skills needed to be successful in school and in life.

The ***Complete STEM Smart*** series is a set of innovative STEM-based workbooks that covers Grade 1 to Grade 6. Each of these resourceful workbooks comprises four major sections: Life Systems, Structures and Mechanisms, Matter and Energy, and Earth and Space Systems. Each section has two parts: Basic Science Concepts and STEM Experiments.

- Basic Science Concepts – introducing grade-appropriate basic science concepts with correlated units to help children build a strong foundation in science

- STEM Experiments – allowing children to experience hands-on learning to develop logical and critical thinking skills, and to make practical connections among science, technology, engineering, and math

Through using our ***Complete STEM Smart*** workbooks, your child will be encouraged to ask questions, make observations, think critically, and explain his or her reasonings. As your child comes across any obstacles through the experiments, he or she will discover that these obstacles can help make the learning experience positive and valuable and understand that it is the key to success.

Furthermore, "Fun to Know" and our bonus online resources with "Trivia Questions" are provided to inspire and motivate your young scientist, technology specialist, engineer, or mathematician through the STEM journey of discovering this world!

Your Partner in Education,
STEM Team at Popular Book Company (Canada) Ltd.

Table of Contents

Section 1: Life Systems

Basic Science Concepts

Unit 1
Biomes p. 10

Unit 2
Habitats and Communities p. 16

Unit 3
Changes to Habitats p. 22

Unit 4
Our Interaction with Habitats p. 28

Unit 5
Food Chains p. 34

Unit 6
What Animals Eat p. 40

STEM Experiments

Experiment 1:
A Bird's Home
p. 46

Experiment 2:
Amazing Builders
p. 50

Experiment 3:
Thank You, Plants!
p. 54

Experiment 4:
Oil-soaked Feathers
p. 58

Experiment 5:
Camouflaged Pipe Cleaners
p. 62

Section 2: Structures and Mechanisms

Basic Science Concepts

Unit 1
Machines in the Past p. 68

Unit 2
Simple Machines p. 74

Unit 3
Gears p. 80

Unit 4
Gears around Us p. 86

Unit 5
Pulleys Everywhere p. 92

Unit 6
Pulley Power p. 98

STEM Experiments

Experiment 1:
Powerful Pulleys
p. 104

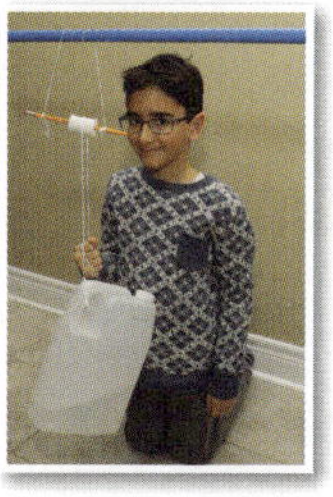

Experiment 2:
A Team of Pulleys
p. 108

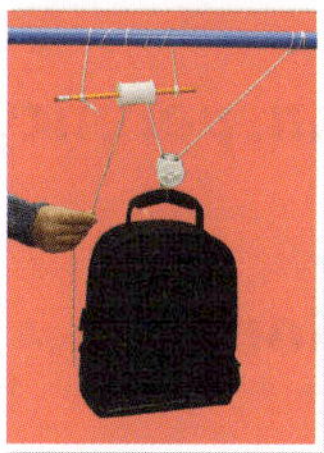

Experiment 3:
Teeth on Gears
p. 112

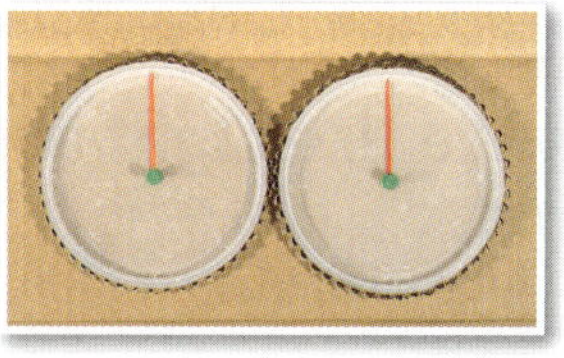

Experiment 4:
Twist and Turn!
p. 116

Section 3: Matter and Energy

Basic Science Concepts

Unit 1
Light around Us p. 122

Unit 2
Light: Reflection and Refraction p. 126

Unit 3
Light: Transparency p. 130

Unit 4
What Is Sound? p. 134

Unit 5
What Happens to Sound p. 138

Unit 6
How We Use Light and Sound p. 142

STEM Experiments

Experiment 1:
Gray Tomatoes
p. 146

Experiment 2:
Light Reflection
p. 150

Experiment 3:
Bending Light
p. 154

Experiment 4:
A CD Spectrometer
p. 158

Experiment 5:
Sound Travels
p. 162

Experiment 6:
Hearing Sounds
p. 166

Experiment 7:
Reflectors and Absorbers
p. 170

Section 4: Earth and Space Systems

Basic Science Concepts

Unit 1
Rocks and Minerals p. 176

Unit 2
Minerals p. 180

Unit 3
Rocks p. 184

Unit 4
The Rock Cycle p. 188

Unit 5
How We Use Rocks p. 192

Unit 6
More about How We Use Rocks p. 196

Answers p. 218

STEM Experiments

Experiment 1:
Volcanoes
p. 200

Experiment 2:
Growing Minerals
p. 204

Experiment 3:
Salt Damage
p. 208

Experiment 4:
Fossilized Rocks
p. 212

Section 1

Life Systems

1 Biomes

Every living thing needs a place that provides the food, water, and space that it needs to survive. We call these homes habitats, and they can be very different from one another. Habitats have different temperatures, water availability, and other factors that make them suited to those that live there.

After completing this unit, you will

- know that a habitat is the most comfortable home for those organisms living in it.
- know that a habitat provides organisms with food, water, air, space, and light.
- understand that there are different types of habitats.

Vocabulary

organism: a form of life considered as a unit such as an animal, a plant, and a fungus

biome: an ecological community, such as a grassland or desert, characterized by its climate and plant life

Extension

Do you know that your backyard is a habitat for many animals and plants, such as snails and weeds? If we build a habitat for those animals or plants, they may love their new home.

Think about the questions below to see what we should consider before creating a habitat for garden snails.

- *Where does a snail like to live?*
- *What does it eat?*
- *Is its habitat sunny or dark, warm or hot, wet or dry?*

Surf the Internet with the permission from an adult or read a book to find out about garden snails and their habitats.

A. Check or circle the correct answers.

Facts about Garden Snails

Habitat

- ◯ in deserts
- ◯ in gardens
- ◯ in oceans
- ◯ in forests

- sunny / dark
- warm / hot
- wet / dry

Diet

- ◯ leaves
- ◯ fruits
- ◯ insects
- ◯ cheese

B. Fill in the blanks to complete the descriptions of different types of biomes. Then circle the organisms that live in these habitats.

insects life grasses camels water permafrost
coldest elephants treeless plankton precipitation
ferns cushion plants blue whale hot

Different Types of Biomes

Grassland

Grasslands in Kenya

Grasslands exist throughout Earth. These biomes are marked by sparse trees, extensive 1. ______________ , and a variety of small and large animals, such as grasshoppers and 2. ______________. There are grazing animals, burrowing animals, and their predators. Insects are abundant.

Desert

Flora of Sonoran Desert in Arizona, U.S.

Many living things thrive in the 3. ______________ , dry desert. Desert plants and animals, such as cacti and 4. ______________ , have interesting features that help them survive in this harsh environment. They both have the ability to collect and store 5. ______________ . There is generally a smaller concentration of life forms in a desert than in other biomes.

Tundra

Tundra in Alaska, U.S.

The tundra is a cold, 6. treeless area; it is the 7. coldest biome. The tundra has very low temperature and very little 8. Precipitation. Below a thin layer of soil is 9. Permafrost, a layer of ground that is frozen all year long. During the short summer, the top section of the soil may thaw just long enough to allow plants to grow. Some types of plants that can take the cold and dry conditions are 10. grasses such as reindeer moss.

Tropical Rainforest

Amazon River rainforest in Peru

Tropical rainforests are found in locations that receive significant amounts of precipitation. Their locations are easily recognizable by their abundance of 11. life forms. These life forms include numerous trees, plants such as 12. cushion plants, and an abundance of 13. insects, spiders, snakes, and other animals.

Ocean

Pacific Ocean off Hawaii, U.S.

This home covers more than half of Earth's surface. The ocean is home to a huge variety of species, from the smallest 14. Plankton to the largest creature on Earth, the 15. blue whale. It contains an incredibly diverse web of life.

C. Read the passage. Then complete the chart.

Rainforests:
Tropical and Temperate

Many think of rainforests as tropical areas close to the equator: always warm and rainy. However, there are rainforests found farther north, too, on the Pacific coast such as Olympic National Park in the State of Washington. Called temperate rainforests, they are far from the equator and cooler than tropical rainforests; these cooler temperatures limit the types of species that can live there. Both types of rainforests, however, share two features: tall trees and high levels of precipitation.

In a tropical rainforest, precipitation is mostly rain. However, in a temperate rainforest, precipitation also includes fog, drizzle, and snow. Both types of rainforests receive a lot of precipitation. For example, the temperate rainforest at Olympic National Park gets an average of about 150 in (about 3,810 mm) of precipitation each year, while tropical rainforests get at least 60 in (about 1,520 mm).

Tropical rainforests are home to millions of species; temperate rainforests are home to only thousands. In the temperate rainforests in the United States, giant coniferous trees dominate, and animals include the black bear, cougar, salmon, and bald eagle. Broad-leaved trees dominate tropical rainforests, and animals in Brazil's Amazon rainforest include the giant anteater, anaconda, and jaguar.

Habitats are found in tundra, grasslands, forests, and deserts, but now you know there are rainforest habitats, too.

Types of Rainforests

Tr opical Rainforest

Location

- close to the equator

Precipitation

- at least 60 in each year

Temperature

- Hot ter than ter

Animal

- Giant anteater, anaconda, and jaguar

Plant

- Broad-leaved trees

Te______ Rainforest

Location

- far from the equator
- on the pacific coast

Precipitation

- 150 in, c 3810 mm

Temperature

- cooler than trr

Animal

- Black bears, cougar, Salmon, and bald eagle.

Plant

- Coniferous tree

2 Habitats and Communities

Plants and animals live together and interact in a common habitat. They depend on their environment and each other to survive. The specific needs of the living things have to be met within their habitat, or they cannot continue to exist there.

After completing this unit, you will

- understand that living things depend on their habitats to meet their basic needs.
- know that some environmental elements affect the ability of living things to survive in a habitat.
- know that the unique features of some living things help them survive in their habitats.

Vocabulary

habitat: the place where a species naturally or normally lives and grows

community: interacting species that share a common habitat

adaptation: a unique feature of a living thing that makes it fit into a specific environment

Extension

Have you ever visited a zoo? Zoos have different exhibits that mimic the natural habitats of animals from around the world. When you visit different exhibits at a zoo, make a record of the animals and plants that can be found there. Then describe the setting of the exhibit to show how it accommodates the needs of the animals and plants.

Tundra Exhibit
(covered with snow, very cold)

Animals: polar bears, arctic foxes, snowy owls

Description: white hairs – blending into the snow

Plants: tiny leaves, growing close to the ground

A. Match each source with what it provides us. Write the letter.

- **A** clothes/bedding
- **B** water
- **C** heat/light
- **D** food
- **E** shelter

sun

vegetables

river

cotton plant

tree

B. Choose the correct descriptions for the habitats. Write the letters. Then match each animal or plant with the habitat it is best suited to.

A *a land that is partly covered with water; always wet*

B *a very dry area that is mostly hot during the day*

C *a place with many trees and abundant food for animals*

D *a place that has sparse vegetation and is cold throughout the year*

E *a big, open space with grass*

Habitat

1. ☐ tundra •
2. ☐ desert •
3. ☐ wetland •
4. ☐ forest •
5. ☐ grassland •

- scorpion
- frog
- monkey
- cactus
- zebra
- mosquito
- snowy owl
- bear
- arctic hare
- grasshopper

C. **Write the unique features of the animals and plants to show how they adapt to their habitats. Then give one more adaptive feature for each of them.**

- *thick, furry coat*
- *webbed feet to swim*
- *hard, pointed beak to crack seeds*
- *thick stem to store water*
- *strong, fast runner*

1.  **wetland** ____________________

____

2.  **forest** ____________________

____

3.  **desert** ____________________

____

4.  **tundra** ____________________

____

5.  **grassland** ____________________

____

D. Read the passage. Then answer the questions.

The giant panda's only natural habitat is China's mountain forests. Pandas prefer to live alone, and the forests give them plenty of room to roam, eat, swim, climb, and sleep. Pandas are very picky eaters. While they do eat other foods, such as insects and grass, they mostly eat bamboo, which is abundant at high altitudes in China's mountain forests. Pandas have strong jaws and large teeth which help them crush the tough bamboo. They are also good climbers, climbing up the mountains to look for food.

The Giant Panda and Its Very Specific Habitat

Unfortunately, pandas' habitat is being destroyed, as people need places to live, work, log, and mine resources. Some animals such as raccoons and foxes can survive, and even thrive, in places where many people live, but pandas cannot adapt. Without a lot of bamboo in their habitat, pandas starve.

For this reason, giant pandas are considered a vulnerable species. Many people are helping giant pandas by working to protect and restore their natural habitat. Hopefully, the giant panda's population will increase with these efforts.

1. What is the giant panda's natural habitat?

(A) tropical rainforests
(B) mountain forests
(C) grasslands

2. What is the giant panda's favorite food?

(A) bamboo
(B) foxes
(C) insects

3. What are the unique features the giant panda has that make it suited for its habitat?

(A) strong jaws and large teeth to crush hard bamboo
(B) a long neck for reaching leaves high up
(C) good at climbing
(D) sharp claws for digging

4.

Give a reason why we are considered a vulnerable species.

____

____

____

____

____

3 Changes to Habitats

When a habitat changes, it affects the organisms living in it. Sometimes, when there are too many changes, the organisms may leave the habitat or die off. In this unit, you will learn that changes to habitats are caused by human activities or natural forces, and learn about some plants and animals that are classified as threatened due to the decline in their populations.

After completing this unit, you will

- learn that changes to habitats can be caused by human activities or natural forces.
- know that there are threatened species around the world.

Vocabulary

deforestation: the process of removing all the trees from an area

threatened species: a species that is vulnerable, endangered, or critically endangered, and may become extinct

gorilla (an endangered animal)

Extension

American ginseng is a valuable plant which has been used as a traditional medicine to prevent colds and boost the immune system. Due to land being cleared for farming and development by builders, the growth of American ginseng has been reduced significantly. Therefore, American ginseng is considered endangered in some states. However, people have been making efforts to save this plant. Hopefully, American ginseng can be removed from the endangered species list one day.

A. Check the actions that could help save American ginseng.

Ⓐ Study the needs of the American ginseng plant to see how it can be reproduced in protected environments.

Ⓑ Dig out all the American ginseng plants and put them in a laboratory.

Ⓒ Block off parts of a development as "ginseng fields" so that no houses can be built in these pockets.

Ⓓ Make a law stating that people can only eat American ginseng during New Year's celebrations.

Ⓔ *Educate people about American ginseng's endangered status so that they use ginseng smartly.*

B. Write "human" for the habitat destructions that are caused by human activities and "natural" for those that are caused by natural forces. Then write the name of each type of destruction.

flooding deforestation farming oil spill wildfire

1.

_______________ ;

____

2.

_______________ ;

____

3.

_______________ ;

____

4.

_______________ ;

____

5.

_______________ ;

____

C. Look at the threatened species. Match the sentences with the correct animals.

Ⓐ I am gigantic. In fact, I am the largest animal in the world!

Ⓑ I love the ice, but it's not always dependable!

Ⓒ I like to travel in a pack and stay awake at night.

Ⓓ I am known for my large beak which I use to crack open seeds and nuts.

Ⓔ I can run over 60 mi (about 100 km) per hour – as fast as a car on the freeway!

Ⓕ People think I am cuddly; it must be my cute, dark eyes. I live in the mountain forests of China.

Threatened Species

1.

2.

3.

4.

5.

6.

D. Read the passage. Then answer the questions.

Climate Change and the Polar Bear

Few species can survive in the Arctic – a land of snow, ice, and frozen ground. Polar bears survive because they have adapted to this habitat with a thick layer of fat keeping them warm and huge, rough paws giving them traction on the ice. Moreover, they use sea ice as a platform from which to hunt seals, waiting at holes in the ice that their strong sense of smell leads them to, until the seals come up for air.

However, their habitat is changing. Due to rising temperatures, sea ice melts earlier each spring. Early ice melt means that polar bears have fewer days to hunt seals, forcing them to eat less while their thick layer of fat shrinks. They may die of hunger or the inability to keep themselves warm, resulting in their decline in population. Polar bears are considered a threatened species.

Many organizations are working to protect polar bears and their habitat. They include World Wildlife Fund and Polar Bears International. Visit their websites to see what you can do to protect polar bears!

1. Find pictures of the Arctic and polar bears and paste them in the boxes. Then fill in the information and answer the question.

The Arctic

Habitat Description:

____

Reason for Habitat Change:

____

Effect on the Environment:

____

Polar Bear

Adaptations:

- _______________________________
- _______________________________

Threats to Survival:

- _______________________________
- _______________________________

2. Name an organization that helps protect the polar bear. Then visit its website to find an example of what it does to protect the polar bear.

____

____

4 Our Interaction with Habitats

We depend on our habitat to provide the essentials of life. We get food, water, clothing, building materials, and medicine from our environment. In this unit, you will learn about interactions between us and our habitat and what we do to lessen the negative impacts of our activities.

After completing this unit, you will

- know that our habitat provides us with the essentials of life.
- understand that a development project has both positive and negative impacts on habitats and communities.
- understand how we try to conserve our resources.

vocabulary

natural resource: a raw material found in nature

ecologist: a scientist who studies the relationship between organisms and their environment

rock (a natural resource)

Extension

Look at the things around you. Do you know where they come from? Our habitat provides us with all the things we need to survive. Trees are a key element in our habitat and they provide us with thousands of products that we use every day. How many different tree products can you find in your home? Below is a list for your reference.

Tree Products

Food
apple
syrup

Beauty
argan oil
shea butter

Furniture
chair
table

Building Materials
lumber
plywood

Others
medicine for treating malaria
fresh air

A. Suggest something for which each natural resource below is used. Then answer the question.

1. diamond

____

2. aluminum

____

3. water

____

4. gold

____

5. wind

____

6. oil

____

7. Name one more natural resource and describe one of its uses.

______________ : ____

B. Read the paragraphs and what the people say. Decide what each person is most concerned about and check that circle. Then answer the question.

The community of South Ferris is growing, and the community leaders propose to build more houses for the expanding population. A new housing development will be built in a woodland area.

A meeting is called so that everyone interested in the development can present their opinions.

1. Mr. Smith, one of the community leaders, says, "We plan to build 1,000 houses for families in need."

   (A) positive impact on the community
   (B) negative impact on the community
   (C) positive impact on the habitat

2. Ms. Brant, a conservationist who is committed to protecting the environment, says, "Thirty acres of natural habitat will be destroyed. The animals will have nowhere to go!"

   (A) positive impact on the community
   (B) positive impact on the habitat
   (C) negative impact on the habitat

3. *The fox family will have to move out of the woodlands because they will no longer be able to find shelter or food. It will have a major impact on wildlife.*

- (A) positive impact on the community
- (B) negative impact on the habitat
- (C) positive impact on the habitat

4. Mr. Bell, a developer, says, "It is a good idea because it will generate more tax revenue for community improvement."

- (A) positive impact on the community
- (B) negative impact on the community
- (C) negative impact on the habitat

5. Check the ways that may help minimize any negative impacts. Then give an idea of your own.

- (A) Expand the community within the existing boundaries.
- (B) Build the new houses with high-quality materials.
- (C) Renovate the old buildings to make good use of already developed spaces.
- (D) Abandon all housing development projects.
- ✔ ______________________________

____

C. Read the passage. Then answer the questions.

The World's First National Park:

Yellowstone National Park

Established in 1872, Yellowstone National Park is the world's first national park. It is located in Wyoming, Montana, and Idaho in the United States and contains many amazing natural wonders, including active geysers, rivers, and canyons. About 400 species of animals, such as elks, wolves, grizzly bears, bald eagles, and wild ducks, call it home. Thousands of plants including lodgepole pines, white spruces, and subalpine firs, and wildflowers can be found in the park. The park protects habitats and wildlife while ensuring that people can enjoy, understand, and appreciate the natural world.

Millions of people visit the park to explore the unique natural wonders and observe wildlife in its intact ecosystem every year. Numerous measures are in effect to protect the park from negative human impacts. Among the many protective measures, one requires visitors with watercraft to have their boats, equipment, and all the gear cleaned, drained, and dried before they arrive in the park and whenever they leave a body of water. This measure helps prevent the spread of aquatic invasive species that could negatively impact the aquatic ecosystem by posing threat to the habitats of the native species and disrupting the food chains in the Greater Yellowstone Ecosystem. With minimal human interference, the ecosystem is able to function and evolve naturally.

1. Search the Internet to find a picture of Yellowstone National Park. Then print and paste the picture in the box.

2. Where is Yellowstone National Park?

____

3. What landforms can be found in Yellowstone National Park?

____

____

4. Name two animals and two plants that call Yellowstone National Park home.

____

____

5. Why is it important to protect the park from negative human impacts?

____

____

5 Food Chains

Plants and animals depend on each other to survive in their surroundings. Each organism is part of the food chain. Energy from the sun helps plants grow, and these plants are then eaten by animals. Each part of the food chain depends on another to get energy.

After completing this unit, you will

- understand that plants use energy from the sun to grow.
- understand that animals get their energy from plants and other animals.
- understand what decomposers do.

The carrot gets energy from the sun; the bunny gets energy from the carrot; and the fox gets energy from the bunny.

Vocabulary

consumers: organisms that feed on plants or animals

producers: organisms that make their own food using energy from the sun

decomposers: organisms that break down dead organic matter into smaller pieces

Extension

Plants need water and nutrients from the soil as well as energy from the sun to make food in order to live and grow. These plants become food for animals which, in turn, provide food for other animals. Without plants, no animals could survive.

What would happen if there were no sun or water to feed plants?

Conditions

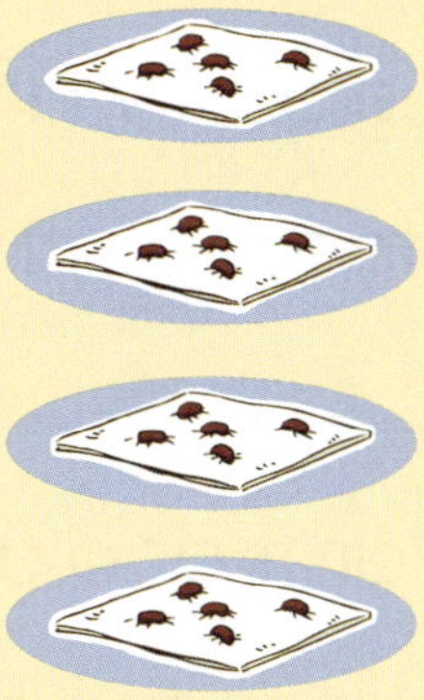

A *water + under the sun*

B *water + in a dark cupboard*

C *no water + under the sun*

D *no water + in a dark cupboard*

After a few days, take a look and see how the seeds respond to these conditions.

A. Look at the extension above. Match the results with the seeds under different conditions. Write the letters.

1.

2.

3. Seeds with no change: ____________

B. Fill in the blanks with the given words. Then write the role of each organism in the food chain.

decomposers producers consumers

Living things in a food chain can be 1. p__________, 2. c__________, or 3. d__________. 4. __________ are plants that make their own food using energy from the sun, water, and air. 5. __________ cannot create their own food, so they get energy by eating animals and plants. 6. __________, such as mushrooms and bacteria, break down dead plants and animals. These decomposed materials are then returned to the soil and they become essential nutrients for plants.

Food Chain

An arrow in a food chain represents a transfer of energy and nutrients from one living thing to another.

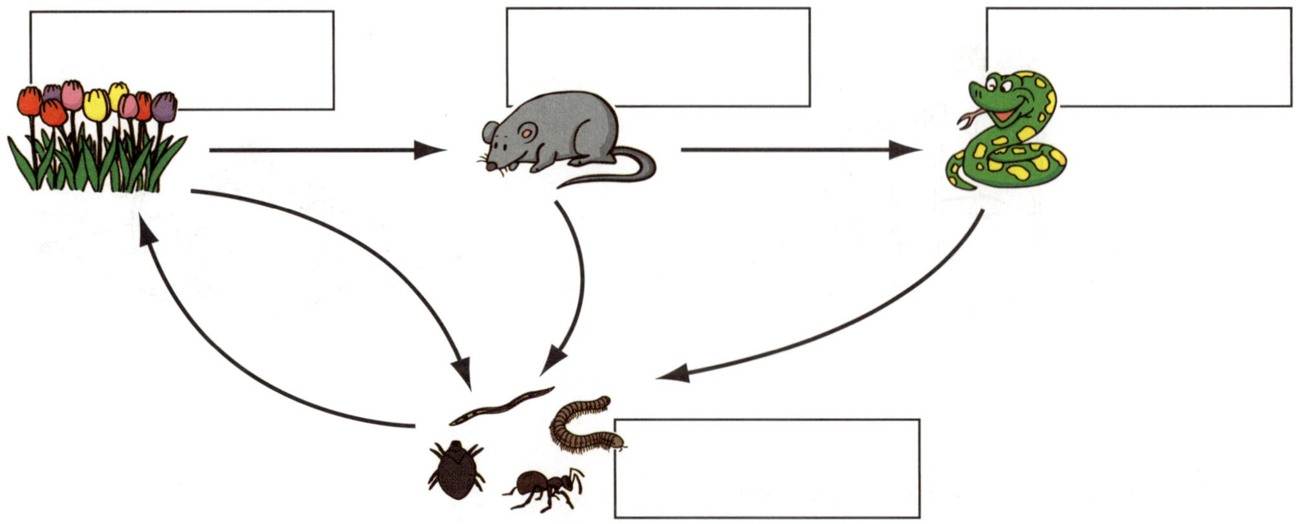

C. Decide whether each organism is a producer, consumer, or decomposer.

A ____________________

B ____________________

C ____________________

D ____________________

E ____________________

D. Fill in the missing animals or plants to complete the food chains. Then build a food chain with the given organisms.

1. grass → ____________ → human

2. ____________ → grasshopper → bird → ____________

3. leaf → caterpillar → ____________ → hawk

4. **polar bear** **arctic cod** **algae** **shrimp** **seal**

Arctic Food Chain ____

____

E. Read the passage. Then answer the questions.

Decomposers: Nature's Recyclers

Decomposers are vital to all food chains. They are nature's recyclers, breaking down dead plant and animal matter into essential nutrients and returning those nutrients to the soil so that producers can use them to make food. Decomposers do their work by producing chemicals, called enzymes, to digest the dead organic matter.

Many decomposers are microorganisms, which can only be seen under a microscope. These decomposers include bacteria, some of which can be found inside our bodies, helping us digest our food, and fungi, which you can see in the form of mushrooms growing on dead trees or as mold growing on old bread. Most worms are also considered decomposers and are a great addition to your backyard compost heap.

Next time you see a piece of forgotten, moldy bread in a dark corner of a cupboard or an earthworm squirming across your front lawn, think about this: without decomposers, dead plant and animal matter would cover our Earth, from forests to sidewalks to your own backyard!

1. Circle the correct words.

   a. Decomposers are **important / not important** to all food chains.

   b. Decomposers produce **waste / enzymes** to digest dead organic matter.

   c. Bacteria are **decomposers / fungi** that are able to break down dead organic matter.

   d. Without decomposers, our Earth would be covered in **nutrients / waste** .

2. Give three examples of decomposers.

   ____

3. Why do decomposers play an important role in all food chains?

   ____

   ____

4. Which of the following are evidence of decomposers at work? Check the correct answers.

   (A) rotten lettuce
   (B) growing sunflowers
   (C) broken glass
   (D) moldy bread
   (E) decaying leaves
   (F) mushrooms growing on dead trees

6 What Animals Eat

Have you seen a cow eat meat or a lion eat grass? Probably not! Different animals have different diets. In this unit, you will learn about how animals can be classified by what they eat – as herbivores, carnivores, or omnivores.

After completing this unit, you will

- know that animals have different diets and that they are classified into three groups accordingly.
- understand that organisms get energy from other organisms through the food chain.

Vocabulary

herbivore: an animal that eats plants only

carnivore: an animal that eats animals only

omnivore: an animal that eats both plants and animals

Extension

Animals have specialized teeth to help them eat. Take a closer look at the teeth of a lion and a giraffe. You can see that lions have sharp and long teeth, called fangs, for tearing meat. These sharp teeth are like knives, which are perfect for lions because they are meat eaters. How about the teeth of a giraffe? Giraffes have big, flat teeth which are perfect for grinding their favorite food – leaves. Giraffes are plant eaters.

Look in a mirror and check your teeth to see what kind you have. Are you a meat eater or plant eater?

A. Check the animals that are meat eaters. Then answer the questions.

1.

2. Name one feature the meat eaters have in common.

____

3. Look at the animals that you did not check. What do they eat?

____

B. Fill in the blanks with the given words to complete the paragraph. Then classify the animals.

herbivores	omnivores	consumers
carnivores	producers	decomposers

1. ____________, mostly plants, are always at the beginning of a food chain. Next are the 2. ____________, which are animals. Based on their eating habits, animals are classified as one of three types of consumers: animals that eat plants are 3. ____________; animals that eat other animals are 4. ____________; and animals that eat both plants and animals are 5. ____________. 6. ____________ are always directly linked to the producer in a food chain.

7. **Types of Animals**

A ____________

B ____________

C ____________

D ____________

E ____________

C. Read what the girl says. Complete the food chain with the given animals and label each of them as an omnivore, a herbivore, or a carnivore. Then answer the questions.

Every level of a food chain gets energy from the level below it and gives energy to the level above it, so every level is dependent on the level below for survival.

1. **bobcat caterpillar bird**

leaf → ________ (herbivore) → ________ (   ) → ________ (   )

2. **lizard grasshopper snake**

grass → ________ (   ) → ________ (   ) → ________ (   )

3. What would happen to the food chains if the producers disappeared?

____

4. Look at the food chain in Question 2. What would happen if the lizard was not there? Explain.

____

____

D. Read the passage. Then answer the questions.

What Makes a Blue Whale Big?

The blue whale is the largest animal on Earth. It can weigh 200 tons, about the weight of 33 elephants! A newborn weighs only about 3 tons, but can gain up to 200 pounds (about 91 kilograms) each day. That is like gaining the weight of a professional basketball player each day!

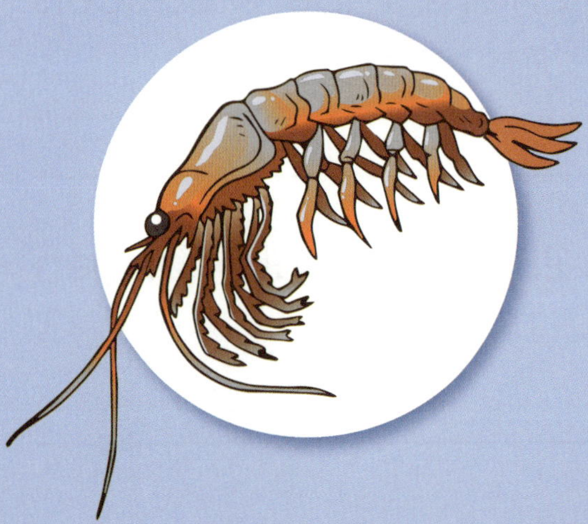

Can you guess what a blue whale eats to get this big? You might think they eat other whales, dolphins, giant fish, squid, or octopuses, but a blue whale's favorite food is a tiny creature called krill. Krill look like shrimp, but most grow to be only the size of a safety pin. An adult blue whale can eat up to 40 million of them a day, bringing huge amounts of krill-filled water into its mouth and filtering it until only krill, and the occasional fish or squid, are left to swallow.

1. Write **T** for true and **F** for false.

a. An elephant weighs as much as 33 blue whales. ______

b. A newborn blue whale weighs about 3 tons. ______

c. A blue whale's favorite foods are dolphins, giant fish, squid, and octopuses. ______

d. Blue whales are carnivores. ______

2. What is the blue whale's favorite food? How much can an adult blue whale eat in a day?

____

____

3. Complete the Antarctic food chain.

krill **plankton** (tiny plants) **blue whale**

__________ → __________ → __________

4. What would happen if plankton were missing in the food chain?

____

____

A BIRD'S HOME

building a nest for a bird's home

Birds and trees live together in a habitat. Birds find homes in trees and eat their fruits. In return, seeds from the fruits are spread to new locations through bird feces and grow into new plants. The relationship between birds and trees is strong and inseparable.

Difficulty:
●●●○○

Time needed:
90 minutes (setup)
2 weeks (observation)

In this experiment, you will understand how birds use natural materials such as leaves, twigs, and grass to build nests for shelter.

STEM Note

Birds' nests serve many purposes. They are places for birds to lay eggs, keep them warm until they hatch, and provide homes for the baby birds as they grow up.

What you need:

twigs

grass

pine needles

leaves

straw

mud

newspaper

cup nest of a common blackbird

What to do:

1. Spread the newspaper over your work surface to help keep the area clean.
2. Use the materials you gathered to build a nest like the nests you saw in your neighborhood or a park. Try to make it as strong as possible.
3. To test your handiwork, try placing it outside on a tree branch or somewhere you think a bird would like to have a nest.
4. Wait a few days or weeks and see if any birds use your nest as their home. Record your observations on the next page.

Was it hard to get all those materials to stick together and make the shape of a nest? Imagine building a nest using just a beak and on the branch of a tree! Isn't it amazing how well birds can build their own homes?

My Record

Location of my bird's nest: ______________________________

Date and Time	No. of Birds Visited	Duration

WHAT *just* happened?

You should have noticed that there are many ways to build birds' nests. In fact, different types of birds build different types of nests, such as cup and cavity nests, to meet their own needs. Cup nests, which are cup-shaped to house the eggs, are the most common nests that we can find in our backyards. Common blackbirds are the experts in building this type of nest. Cavity nests are chambers in living or dead wood. Some birds, like owls, enjoy living in natural cavities, and some birds, like woodpeckers, have strong beaks to help build cavity nests for themselves.

STEM INQUIRY

- What other animals build their own homes?
- Do all animals build shelters for themselves?
- Where can you find birds' nests? What factors do birds consider when selecting the best nesting locations?
- How are nests in warm climates different from nests in colder climates?

- Go online with the permission from an adult and look up photos of different types of birds' nests. Compare them. How are they different?
- Researchers and engineers have designed all types of artificial nests for supporting bird populations, especially for endangered birds. Do some research online with an adult's permission and make nests specifically for birds living in your area with eco-friendly materials. Help promote local biodiversity and contribute to wildlife preservation efforts.

- If you were a bird, how would you structure your nest to ensure it could withstand various weather conditions? What materials would you use?
- Birds and many other animals do not have hands to build with. Try building a nest with tweezers. Was this hard to do?

- There are 3 cup nests in each of the 2 trees. If each cup nest houses 4 eggs, how many eggs are there in total?

AMAZING BUILDERS

understanding how beaver dams are built and their impacts

Beavers are amazing builders. They are capable of building their own dams and lodges using resources in their habitats. Although these structures benefit beavers and some plants and animals, they can also disrupt and impact the environment in a negative way.

STEM Note

Below are some materials beavers use to make a beaver dam.

- for framework: branches, twigs, logs
- for mending: rocks, mud, vegetation

Difficulty:
●●●○○

Time needed:
1 hour

In this experiment, you will explore how beavers build dams.

What you need:

- a large aluminum tray
- rocks
- twigs
- water
- leaves
- sticks
- modeling clay

What to do:

1. Make a row of rocks in the middle of the tray.

2. Place twigs and sticks on top of the rocks to build a dam. Fill up any holes with leaves and modeling clay.

3. Pour water on one side of the dam and observe.

4. Make adjustments to your design such as using more twigs and interweaving the leaves and twigs to find out what works best to keep the water on only one side of your dam.

WHAT *just* happened?

Through this experiment, you should have experienced the construction work that beavers do to build dams out of natural materials. The natural materials that you put together on the tray modeled a beaver dam.

Much of the water stayed on one side of the dam, just like how a beaver dam blocks and diverts the water flowing down from a stream to create a pond on the other side of the dam. The slow-flowing water in the pond creates a perfect environment for beavers to build their lodge. The lodge will give them shelter, warmth, protection, eating areas, as well as storage for food.

Beavers are natural engineers and they know where and how to build their homes with their unique physical features. Inspired by these smart creatures, our engineers replicate beaver dams and build dams for our reservoirs and hydroelectric plants. Think about the amazing structure of the beaver dam, and perhaps you will come up with more brilliant ideas of using them in your innovative designs.

STEM INQUIRY

- What animals are affected by beaver dams?
- Can beaver dams affect humans?
- What does a beaver use its tail for?
- Where does a beaver get the materials to build dams?
- What other mammals build their homes near the water?

- Like beavers, humans have also learned to build dams. Hydroelectric dams wall off water to create reservoirs, which can be used to generate electricity. Do some research online with the permission from an adult to learn more about hydroelectric dams. Where is the closest hydroelectric dam to your home? How many homes does it provide electricity to?
- Civil engineers are professionals who design, plan, and build structures. Research online with an adult's permission to find out what is the scope of work of civil engineers in the public sector.

- How do beavers determine the best locations to build their dams? What factors do you think they consider?

Fun to know

Beavers' Homes

Canadian beavers have built the world's largest beaver dam, which is about 2790 feet (about 850 meters) long, at the southern edge of Wood Buffalo National Park in Alberta, Canada. This great dam showcases the incredible power of nature and the impressive capabilities of these hardworking animals.

THANK YOU, PLANTS!

understanding how plants prevent soil erosion

Plants play a vital role in an ecosystem. Not only do plants provide food and shelter, they also prevent the soil from getting eroded by wind and water. Do this experiment to find out how.

Difficulty: ●●●●○

Time needed:
2 – 4 weeks

In this experiment, you will learn how plants help prevent soil erosion.

What you need:

- a baking sheet
- 2 big plastic bottles
- scissors
- soil
- grass seeds
- tape
- 2 small cups
- water

What to do:

1. Cut open the sides of the bottles. Tape them on the baking sheet with the mouths resting over the rim of the sheet.
2. Add an equal amount of soil to each bottle. In Bottle A, mix in a handful of grass seeds.
3. Place the sheet near a window to receive sunlight. Water the soil in both bottles every day. Go to the next step when the grass is about 2.5 in (about 6 cm) tall.
4. Blow hard on the soil in both bottles. Observe the movements of the soil.
5. Place a small cup under each mouth.
6. Pour the same amount of water into both bottles. Screw off the caps. Compare the water collected.

Soil erosion is an inevitable phenomenon that occurs naturally. However, human activities such as deforestation significantly speed up the rate of soil erosion.

WHAT *just* happened?

The soil in Bottle A was able to withstand the "wind" better compared to the soil in Bottle B. Also, the water collected from Bottle A was clearer than the water from Bottle B.

Soil erosion occurs when soil gets washed away by the forces of wind and water, as demonstrated in Bottle B, in which the soil was easily carried away by the "wind" and water. However, this is not the case with the soil in Bottle A, where there were plants.

Plants play a crucial role in protecting the soil and they do this through their powerful roots. The roots grow deep into the soil, creating a strong and intertwined network. These roots act like a web, gripping the soil to keep it together. When wind blows or water flows, the roots of plants hold onto the soil tightly, providing stability and prevents the soil from being carried away. That is why the soil in Bottle A, with the presence of plants, was able to resist erosion. This experiment shows us one of the many reasons why plants are essential for our environment and the health of our land.

STEM INQUIRY

- What is soil erosion?
- What natural factors contribute to soil erosion?
- What human activities can lead to soil erosion?
- What are some characteristics that make certain plants more effective at controlling soil erosion compared to others? Consider the root depth, root structure, growth speed, etc.

- Environmental conditions should be considered when choosing the best plants for preventing soil erosion in certain areas. Plants that thrive at riverbanks are better at controlling water erosion. Drought-tolerant plants can be used in arid regions. Check online with the permission from an adult to find more information on native plants suitable for erosion control in different environments.

- Can you think of more ways to stabilize the soil in Bottle A and prevent erosion?

- Scientists use the Universal Soil Loss Equation to predict soil loss by water erosion in tons per acre per year. How many square feet is an acre? How many square meters is an acre?

Fun to know

Cover Crops

Cover crops are plants grown to control soil erosion. These plants are usually very hardy, with nets of roots that hold topsoil in place. They protect the soil from being washed away by rain. When planting cover crops, it is best to consider native plants. Native plants will require less maintenance and will thrive in their habitat. Also, consider planting multiple species to improve diversity.

OIL-SOAKED FEATHERS

understanding how oil spills affect birds

Oil spills not only have a negative impact on marine life, but they also threaten the lives of birds that spend most of their time at sea or near the water. When oil spills occur, birds that come into contact with the oil often get contaminated and sick, and unfortunately, most of them will die as a result. Because birds are vulnerable to oil, people have to prevent oil spills from happening.

What you need:

oil

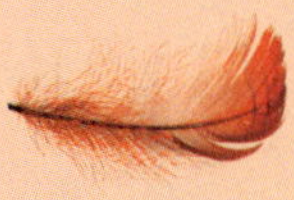

a feather

cold tap water

2 large bowls

STEM Note

Feathers can carry germs and parasites that can make us sick. In some regions, some bird species are protected by the law, and collecting their feathers without appropriate permits can be illegal.

Difficulty: ●○○○○

Time needed: 1 hour

In this experiment, you will explore how oil spills affect birds.

What to do:

1. Add cold tap water to the two bowls.
2. Add some oil to one of the bowls to simulate an oil spill.
3. Dip the feather into the oil spill.
4. Dip the feather in the bowl of clean water and move it back and forth to wash off the oil on the feather. Do not touch or rub the feather with your hands. Just let the water do the cleaning.
5. Let the feather dry. How does the feather look now?

WHAT *just* happened?

You should have noticed that the oil-soaked feather clumped together and remained sticky, greasy, and slimy even after being washed in water. This is because water could not wash off the oil on the feather.

Birds' feathers are naturally light and fluffy, providing birds good insulation and ensuring their smooth flight. However, when birds' feathers are covered by oil, they become soggy and heavy, losing all their functions. Feather clumping creates bare spots on birds' skin, leaving them poorly insulated from heat and cold. It also makes it difficult for birds to balance and fly properly because their wings cannot move freely, especially with the added weight.

Normally, birds have natural oils in their feathers that help repel water, keeping them dry and warm. But when oil covers the feathers, it can be uncomfortable and even dangerous for the birds, as oil-soaked feathers cannot protect them anymore. To make matters worse, as birds try to clean off the oil using their beaks, they may accidentally ingest the toxic oil, making them sick or even die.

That is why it is important to help birds when they encounter oil spills and to keep our environment clean to protect them and other wildlife.

STEM INQUIRY

- What are some other animals that are affected by oil spills?
- What are some other ways birds are affected by oil spills?
- Birds have feathers. What other characteristics do birds have that make them special?
- What are some other human activities that are harmful to plants and animals?

- What can you use to absorb oil that is in water?
- What can you do to prevent oil and other pollutants from getting into oceans, lakes, and rivers?

- For the experiment, if you start drying the feather at 3:25 and it takes 45 minutes for it to dry completely, at what time will the feather be dry?

Fun to know

Cleaning Birds

As you have learned, birds are vulnerable to oil spills. In fact, without our help, most oil-contaminated birds die. Fortunately, there are professional organizations that carry out cleaning operations targeted at oil-coated birds. In these facilities, rescuers will first calm the stressed birds. Then they will wash them in warm soapy water, feed them, and assess the birds' health before returning them to their habitats.

bird not covered in oil

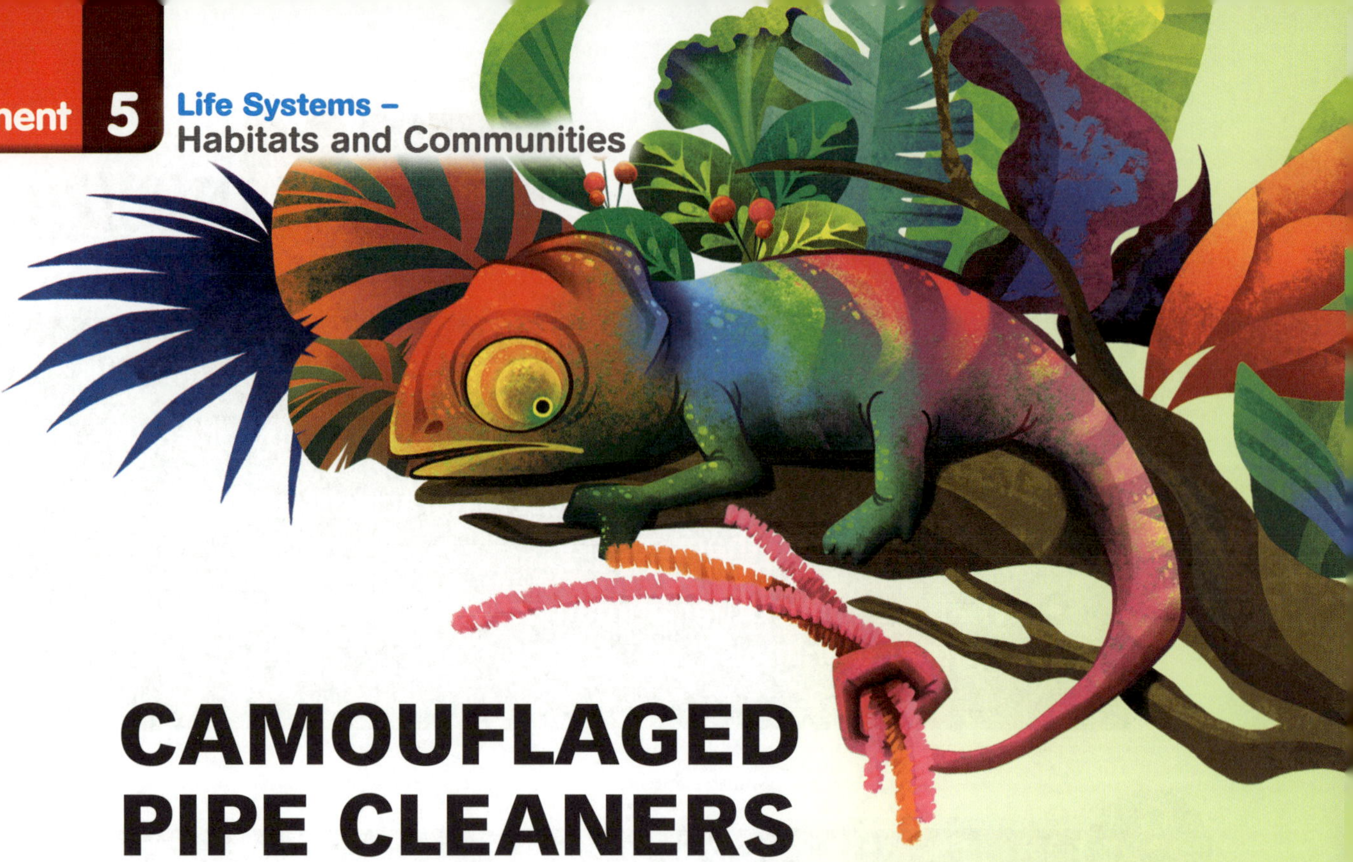

CAMOUFLAGED PIPE CLEANERS

understanding how camouflage helps animals survive

Animals strive to survive in the wild. Camouflage is one of the tricky ways animals blend themselves into their environment to make it difficult for their prey or predators to detect them. Chameleons have the ability to change their colors to match their surroundings when needed. This change of color helps them hide and stay safe. Try this experiment to see how color camouflage works.

What you need:

18 pipe cleaners
- 3 red
- 3 green
- 3 yellow
- 3 brown
- 3 black
- 3 white

string

a big bowl

a timer

What to do:

1. Cut the pipe cleaners into pieces that are about 1 in (about 2.5 cm) long.
2. Mix all the pieces in the bowl.
3. Make a circle with the string on the grass in your backyard.
4. Spread the pieces evenly in the enclosed area.
5. Set the timer for 20 seconds.
6. Go into the circle and pick up as many pieces as you can in 20 seconds.
7. Record the results.
8. Repeat this experiment twice.
9. Compare the results.

Difficulty:

●●○○○

Time needed:
1 hour

In this experiment, you will see how camouflage helps animals hide.

My Record

Number of Pipe Cleaners Picked Up

Trial	Red	Green	Yellow	Brown	Black	White
1						
2						
3						

WHAT *just* happened?

Through several trials, you should have noticed that you picked up fewer green pieces compared to pieces of other colors. This is because the green pipe cleaners blended into the green grass, making it difficult to spot them.

In nature, prey camouflage to hide themselves from their predators to stay safe. For example, grasshoppers have green bodies to blend in with the grass so that their predators may not find them as quickly. Similarly, predators also camouflage to avoid detection by their prey while hunting. Green tree snakes can easily hide themselves in trees to hunt their foods, such as birds and lizards, before they are noticed by their prey.

STEM INQUIRY

- If this experiment is conducted on snow, which color of pipe cleaners do you think you will pick up the least of? Why?
- What are some other animals that you know use camouflage for self-defense or hunting?

- Do you think zebras' black-and-white stripes stand out? Do the stripes provide them camouflage? Research online with the permission from an adult to find out.
- Some animals demonstrate camouflage by changing color, while some by changing smell. Research online with an adult's permission to find out what animals use smell as camouflage.
- Next time you go on camping or hiking, try camouflage yourself using some leaves and sticks. You can even paint on you face. Take photos of yourself and the surroundings to see if you are well camouflaged.

- Scientists have been developing structures and materials that camouflage. What do you think are the purposes or uses of these structures and materials?

- You did the experiment three times. What is the average number of pipe cleaners of each color you picked up? Make a bar graph to show your results.
- For each trial, find the total number of pipe cleaners you picked up in 20 seconds. Then find the rate. Compare the results. Do you notice any improvement as you repeat each trial?

Section 2

Structures and Mechanisms

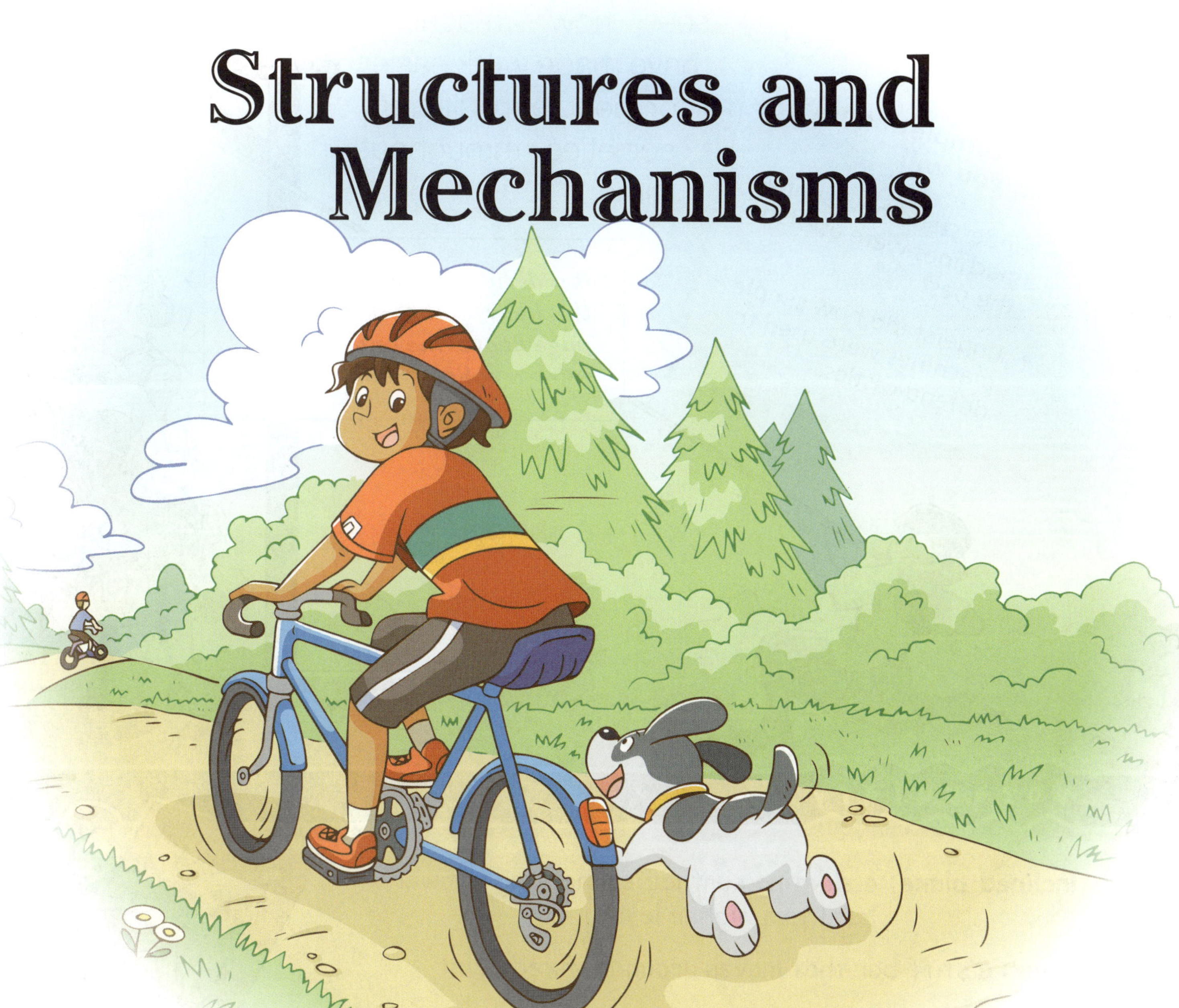

1 Machines in the Past

People have been using simple machines for a long time. During the Middle Ages, simple machines were used to build, protect, and attack medieval castles. In this unit, you will see how machines have made work easier for people in different societies throughout time.

After completing this unit, you will

- understand how simple machines were used in the past.
- understand how simple machines were used to defend castles.

Vocabulary

inclined plane: a slanting surface connecting a lower level to a higher level

lever: a stiff bar that moves around a fixed point

fulcrum: a point on which a lever pivots

wheel: a circular machine that turns around an axle

Extension

An inclined plane is an interesting simple machine because it is simply a flat surface raised at an angle, but it is used in different forms and for various purposes. A ramp is an example of an inclined plane that helps in lifting and moving heavy objects with less effort. Some scientists also believe that an internal ramp system was used to build the Egyptian pyramids.

Nowadays, people have different machines such as slides, roller coasters, stairs, and windmills that use inclined planes. Can you find more examples of inclined planes around you?

A. Unscramble the letters to name the early simple machines. Then fill in the blanks.

1. 

Simple machine: __________ plane
(dnincile)

Moving a heavy load up an inclined plane is __________ than lifting it up.
(easier/harder)

2. 

Simple machine: __________ and __________
(ehwel) (lxae)

It is much __________ to move a heavy load on wheels than dragging it over the ground.
(easier/harder)

B. Complete the passage and label the diagram with the given words. Then put the pictures in order.

sling rope fulcrum lever weight rock

How a Trebuchet* Works

The 1. ______________ of a trebuchet is a long beam fixed at a point called the 2. ______________ . A weight is hung on one end of the beam. A very strong piece of material made into a 3. ______________ is attached on the other end.

Soldiers in the past put a large 4. ______________ inside the sling and used 5. ______________ to pull down this side of the long beam. When it was let go, the heavy 6. ______________ crashed down. This made the other end of the lever fly up, throwing the rock toward a castle.

*A trebuchet was a simple machine that used a lever to shoot a rock into the air to break a castle wall during an attack.

7.

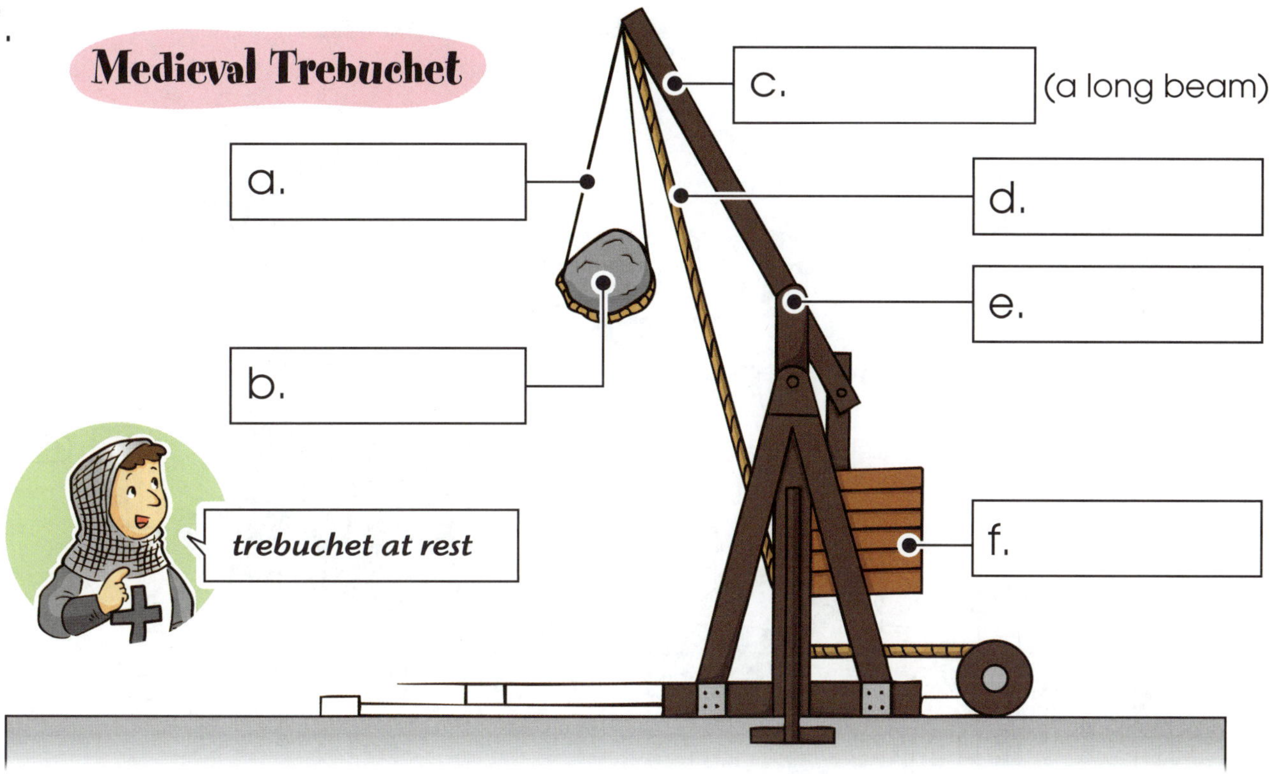

8. Put the pictures in order from 1 to 4 to show how a trebuchet works.

a.

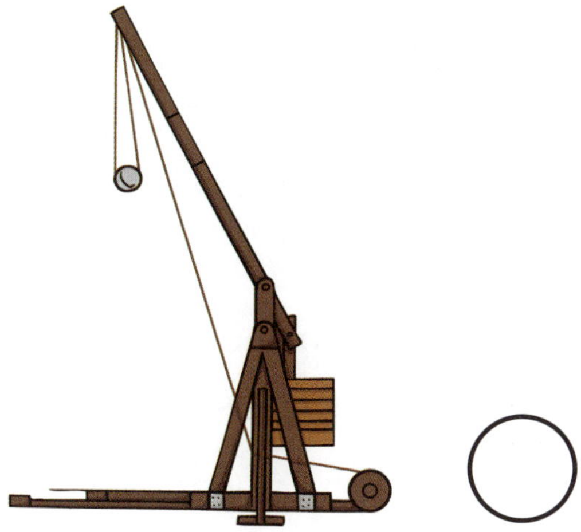

b.

c.

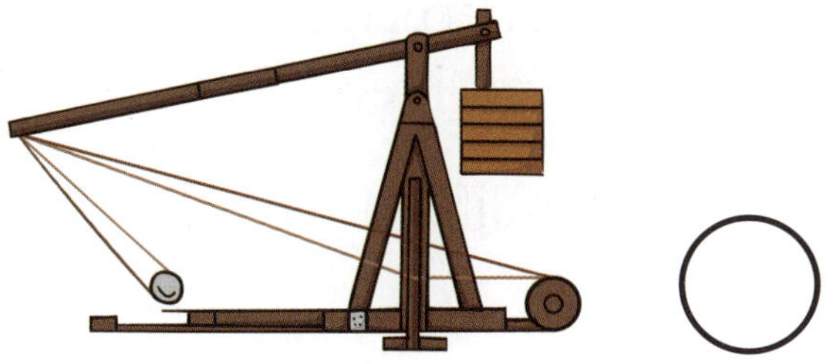

d.

C. Read the passage. Then answer the questions.

Castle Drawbridge – a Simple Machine

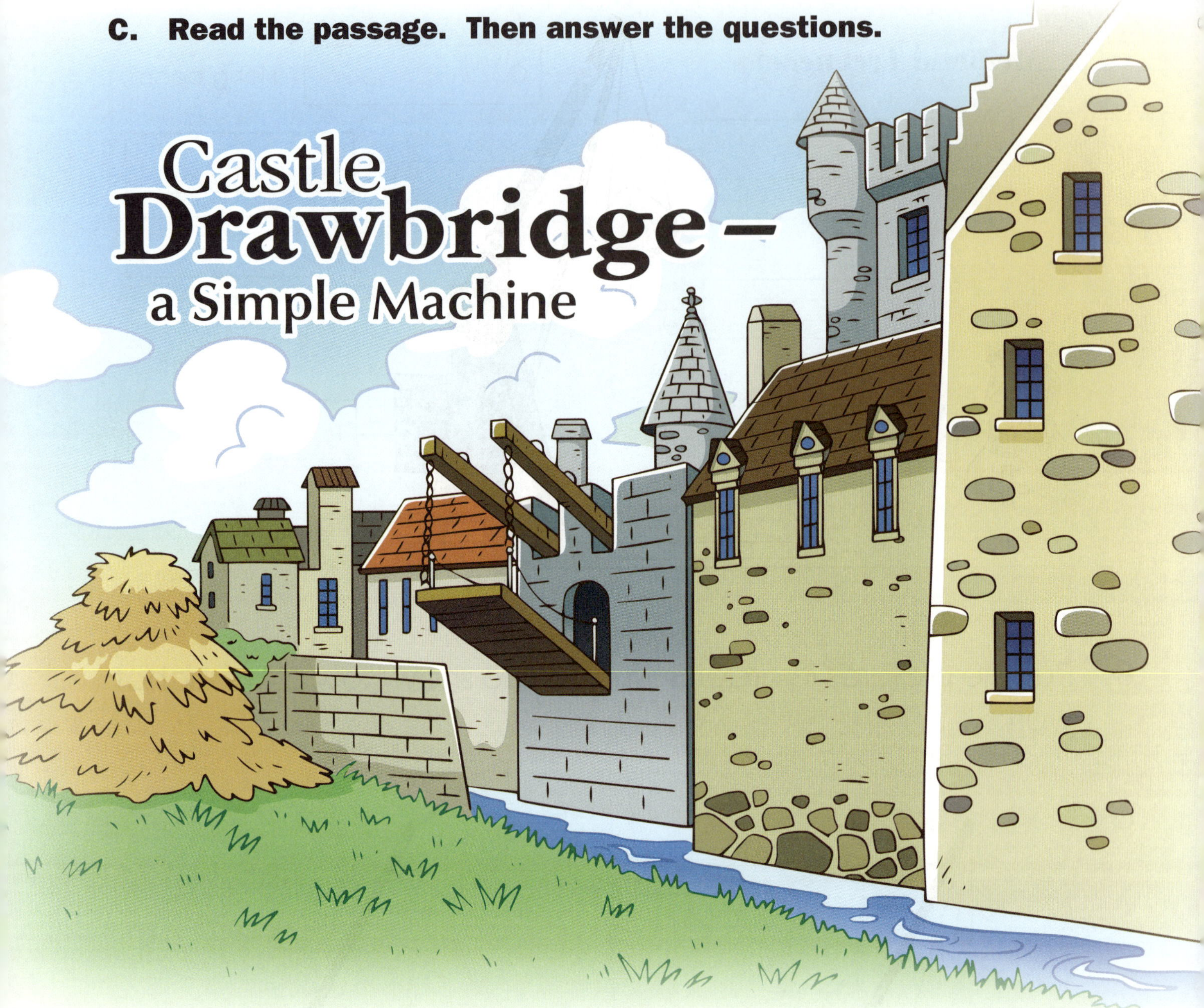

The castle drawbridge was lowered to allow people into the castle through its single entrance and raised to keep attackers out during a siege.

Most worked by using two long pieces of wood, which were levers. They hung above the drawbridge, attached to it by ropes (or by much stronger and longer-lasting chains). Each one was fixed at the castle wall, which was the fulcrum. Behind the castle wall, ropes (or chains) were attached to these pieces of wood. When guards pulled on the ropes, the bridge was lifted.

Weights were also attached to the lever, which made lifting the heavy bridge easier.

1. Label the drawbridge diagram with the given words.

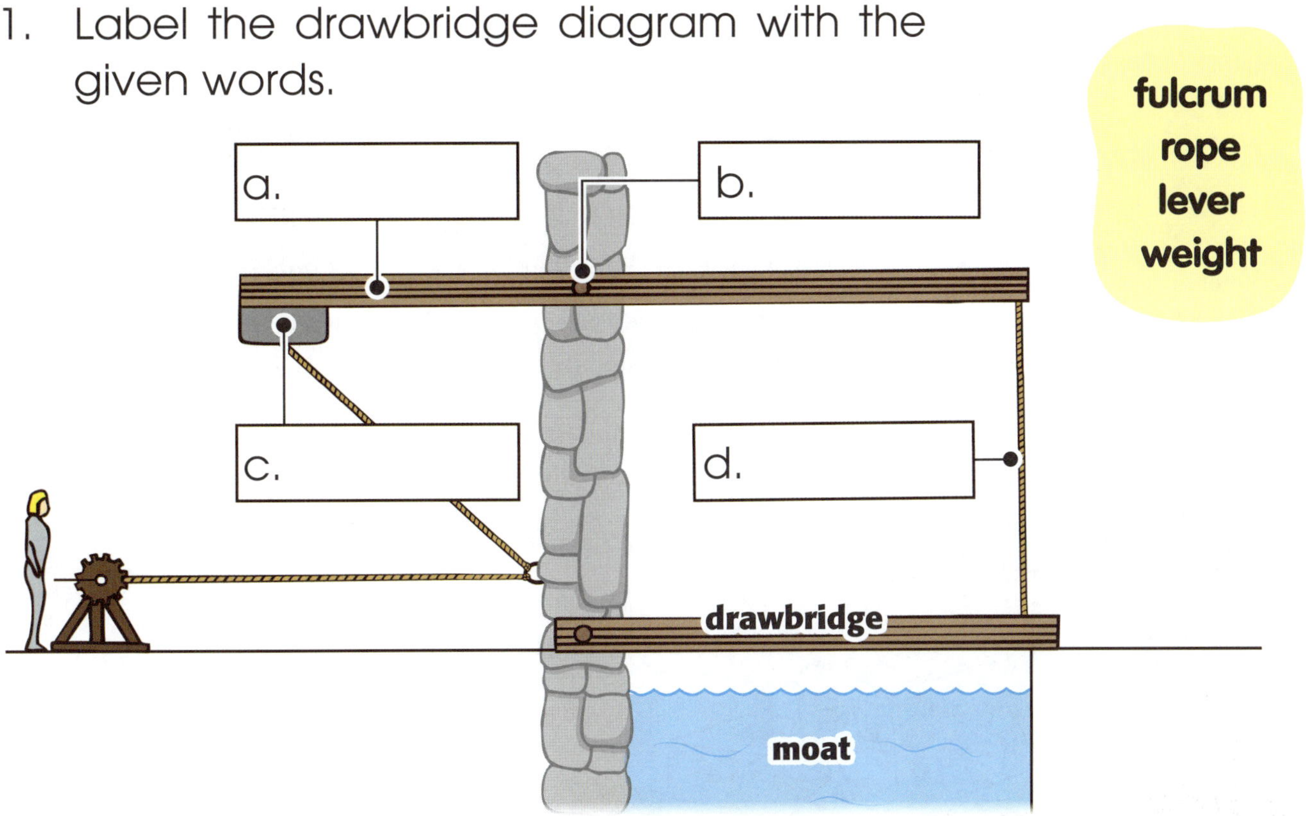

2. Draw the weight, lever, ropes, and drawbridge to show a drawbridge being raised. Then draw arrows to show the direction of the lever's movement.

How a Drawbridge Works

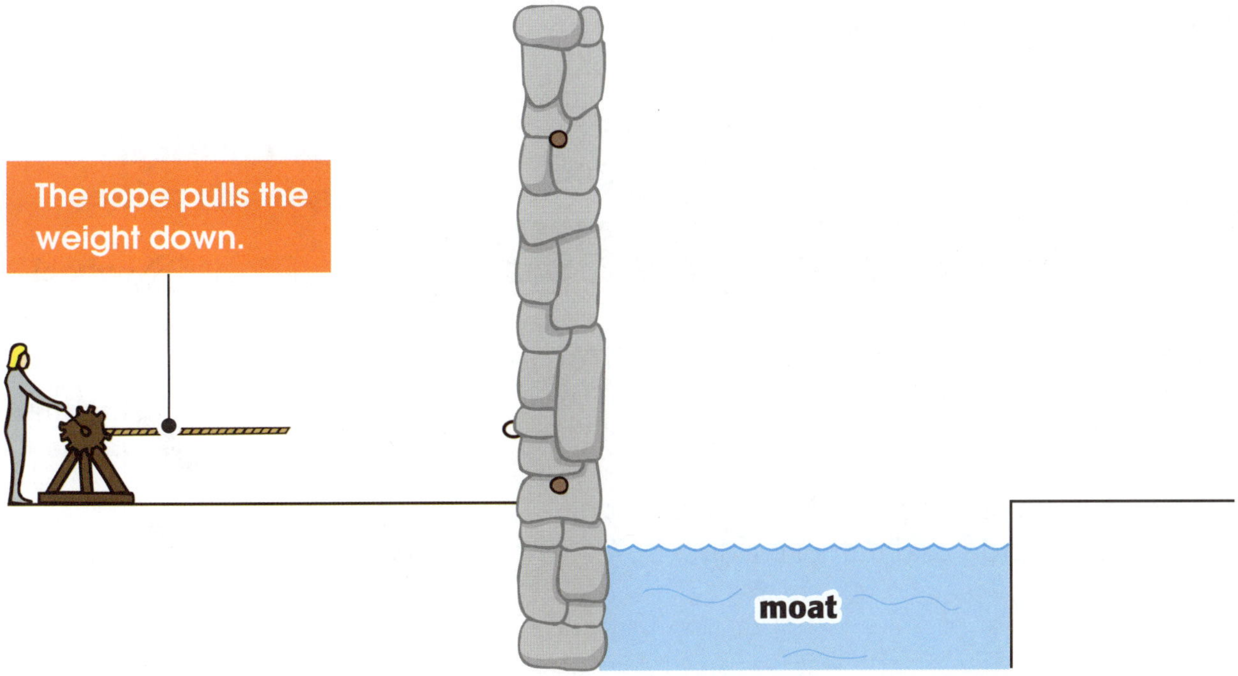

2 Simple Machines

Machines can be very complex, with many moving parts. They can also be simple, with few or no moving parts. These are known as simple machines. In this unit, you will see how simple machines multiply our force and how they help make our work easier.

After completing this unit, you will

- know some safety rules to follow when working with simple machines.
- understand the ways in which some simple machines work.

Six Classical Simple Machines

Vocabulary

simple machine: a device that changes the direction or magnitude of a force

wedge: a simple machine with at least one slanting side and a sharp edge

Extension

Have you ever wondered why it is easy to cut things with knives and saws? When you take a closer look at knives and saws, you may find that they are simple machines – wedges. A wedge has a wide end and a sharp end which work together to split things.

Mom, I know that a sharp knife is safer than a dull one. A dull knife can be much harder to control than a sharp one because we must use more force to cut things with it.

A. Check the safety rules that we should follow when we work with machines.

Safety Rules to Follow When We Work with Machines:

(A) Tie long hair back.

(B) Keep yourself busy at all times.

(C) Wear safety goggles and protective clothing if needed.

(D) Remove loose jewelry.

(E) Wear bright-colored shoes.

(F) Make sure pulleys and gears are fastened securely before testing them with a load.

B. Read the experiments and guess what will happen. Circle the correct answers.

1. **Pulling Power**

A

Get two friends to pull two brooms apart while you try to keep the brooms together.

B

Thread a rope around the two brooms. Get two friends to try to pull the brooms apart while you pull the free end of the rope to keep the brooms together.

Result

A You are **able / unable** to keep the brooms together.

B You are **able / unable** to keep the brooms together.

Conclusion

When the rope is threaded around the brooms, it acts as a group of **pulleys / screws** . The more times the rope loops back and forth, the **greater / smaller** the force is magnified. Therefore, your force in B was **increased / decreased** by the "pulleys."

2. **Gearing up**

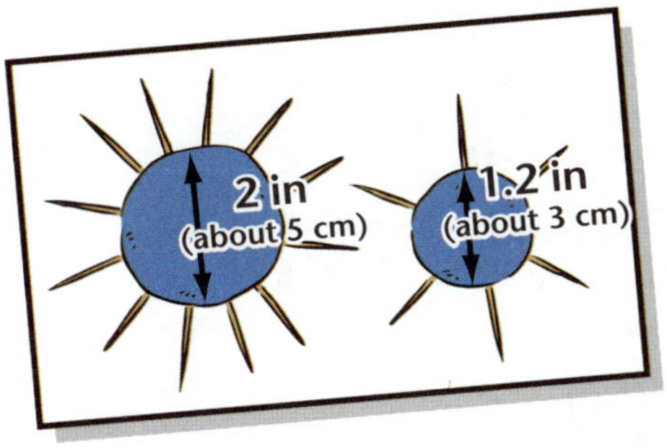

- Flatten two pieces of modeling clay to make two wheels – one 2 in (about 5 cm) across and the other 1.2 in (about 3 cm) across.
- Stick 12 toothpicks evenly around the edge of the big wheel and 6 toothpicks around the small one.
- Push a pencil through the middle of each wheel.
- Squeeze the clay tightly around the pencil so that both the wheel and the axle turn together.
- Place both wheels flat on a table so that their toothpicks interlock.
- Use the pencil to spin the large wheel in a clockwise direction.

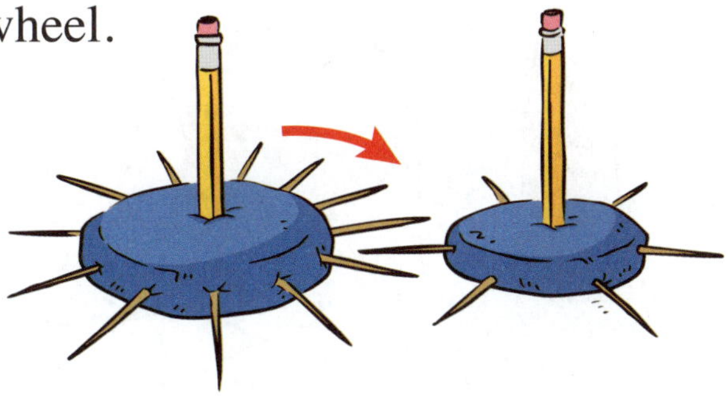

Result

The small wheel spins in a **clockwise / counterclockwise** direction when the big wheel spins in a clockwise direction.

The small wheel spins **faster / slower** than the big one.

Conclusion

The toothpicks are like the teeth on a wheel. Interlocking toothed wheels of different sizes causes the wheels to move at different **speeds / angles** .

The **small / large** wheel makes more turns each time the large wheel turns. Therefore, when we spin the large wheel, the small wheel will move at a **faster / slower** speed.

C. Read the passage. Then answer the questions.

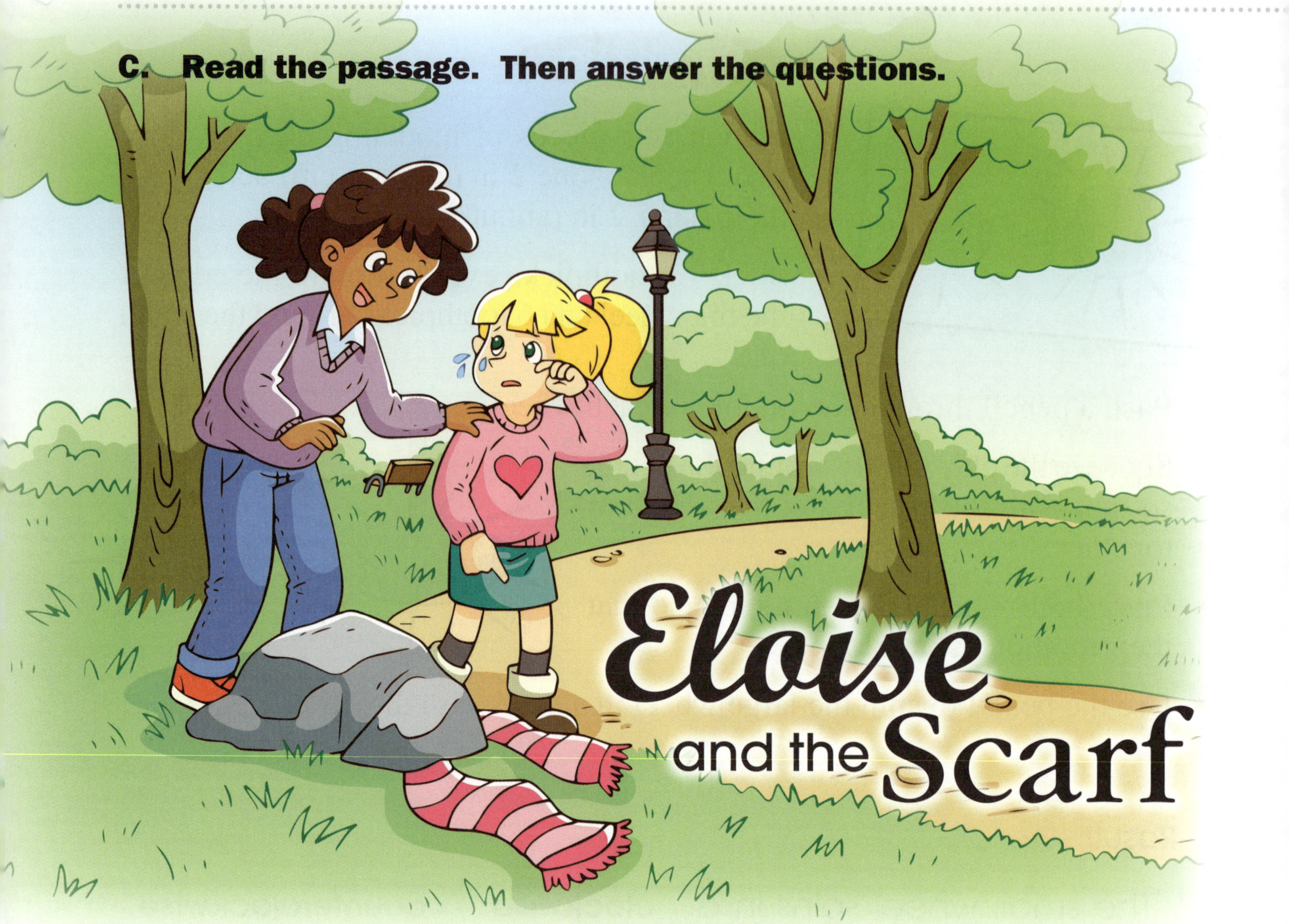

Eloise and the Scarf

Eloise is strolling through the park when she notices a girl crying. "What's wrong?" she asks. The girl cries, "I lost my scarf, and when I found it, it's stuck under this rock!" Eloise knows she can help. She finds a small rock and sets it close to the big rock. Next, she finds a long stick. She puts the stick between the ground and the big rock and rests it on the small rock so that the stick slants upward. She pushes down on the end of the stick, but nothing happens. Then she finds a longer stick and tries again. This time, she lifts the big rock and it rolls away. The girl picks up her scarf. "Thank you," she says. "You're welcome, but you should thank levers*," Eloise laughs.

*lever: a rigid bar that moves around a fulcrum to transfer a force from one place to another

1. Check the picture that shows how Eloise retrieved the scarf from the rock. Then describe each element in the picture with the terms that we use for levers.

A

B

Description: ______________________________

____

____

2. Check the correct sentences.

A You can move a heavy weight with little effort when you use a lever.

B You need to apply more effort over a longer distance to move a load with a lever.

C The longer a lever is, the greater the force it can transfer from the effort to the load.

3. Give an example of a machine that contains the two simple machines given to make our work easier.

a. lever and wedge ______________

b. lever and gears ______________

3 Gears

Do you ride a bicycle? Bike handlebars, pedals, and the wheels and axles are parts you should be familiar with. A bike also has special, toothed wheels called gears that transfer your effort to the bicycle's movement. In this unit, you will learn about how gears work and see how a gear system on a bicycle works.

After completing this unit, you will

- understand how a simple gear train works.
- understand how gears help power bicycles.

Vocabulary

speed: a measure of the rate of motion

force: the capacity to do work or cause physical changes

gear: a toothed machine part that interlocks with another toothed part to transmit motion, or to change speed or direction

Extension

Do you know that there are many things around us that use gears? Gears can be found in everything from cars to clocks. With the help of an adult, check the listed items in your home to see whether or not they use gears.

Items with Gears:

- ◯ clock
- ◯ can opener
- ◯ computer
- ◯ eggbeater

A. Follow the directions to make cardboard gears. Use them to try out the activities in this unit.

1. Trace the gears onto a white sheet of paper.
2. Use this as a stencil to make three big gears (16-tooth) and two small gears (8-tooth) out of heavy, thick cardboard.
3. Cut out the cardboard gears. Ask an adult for help if needed.

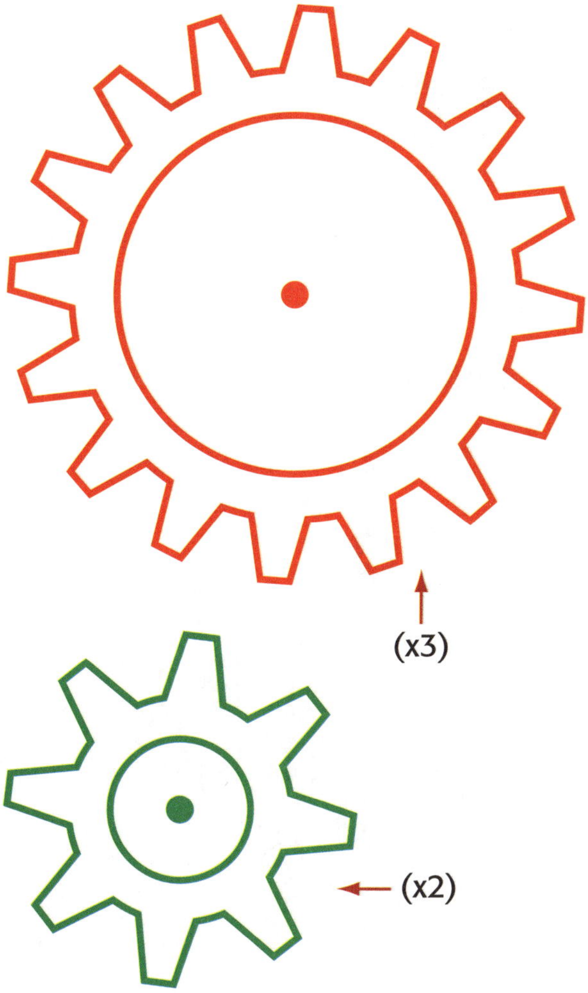

B. Set up and label the 16-tooth gears as shown in the activities below. Then draw arrows to show the directions and answer the questions.

Activity 1

Use brass fasteners to fasten the gears onto a piece of cardboard; make sure the gears interlock.

1. a.

Ⓐ turns clockwise

Ⓑ turns a. ____________________

b.

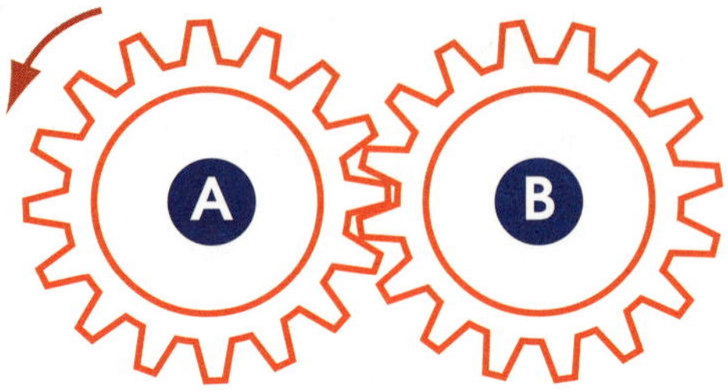

Ⓐ turns counterclockwise

Ⓑ turns b. ____________________

2. Can a gear change the direction of motion? __________

Activity 2

3.

Gear	A	B	C
Direction	↻		
	↺		

4. If another gear is attached to Gear C, in what direction will it turn when Gear A turns clockwise?

____

C. Set up the gears as below. Explore what happens when gears of different sizes are used together. Then answer the questions.

Activity 1

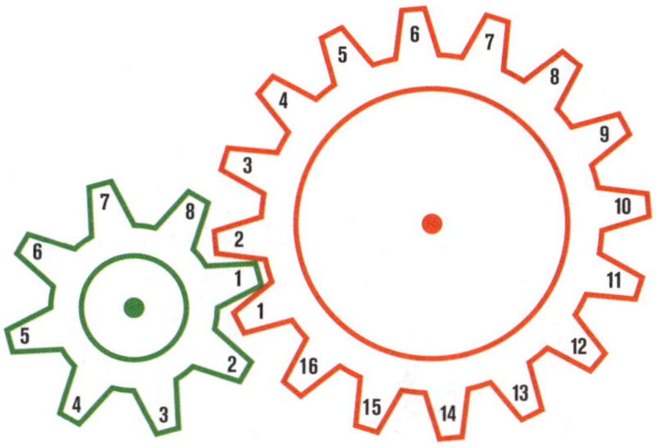

Activity 2

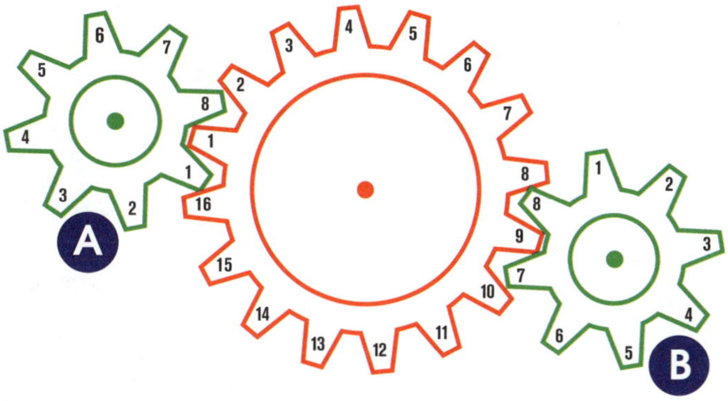

Activity 1 *The big gear turns once in a clockwise direction.*

1. How many times does the small gear turn? ____________

2. Is the speed of the small gear faster or slower than the big gear? ____________

3. In what direction does the small gear turn? ____________

Activity 2 *The big gear turns once in a counterclockwise direction.*

4. How many times does Gear B turn and in what direction?

____

5. Are the speeds of Gears A and B the same? Do they move in the same direction?

____

____

D. Read the passage. Then answer the questions.

A Bicycle's Gears

Pedaling a bicycle makes it move; pedaling is the input component, and the rear wheel's movement is the output component. How does pedaling turn the rear wheel? It is done with gears! Pedals are attached to a front gear, which is connected to a rear gear by a chain. The rear gear is attached to the rear wheel. That is why when a biker pedal, the rear wheel turns.

Most bicycles have front and rear gears of different sizes that are changed for different situations. For **biking on level ground**, a front gear with more teeth (e.g. 50 teeth) and a rear gear with fewer teeth (e.g. 15 teeth) are best. This way, each turn of the pedals rotates the rear wheel more than once, making the bicycle move quickly, though lots of leg strength is needed. For **biking uphill**, a front gear with fewer teeth (e.g. 20 teeth) and a rear gear with more teeth (e.g. 35 teeth) are best. This way, the biker turns the pedals more often for each full rotation of the rear wheel, making it easy to pedal, though difficult to move quickly.

1. Write **T** for true and **F** for false.

a. Pulleys make a bicycle move. ________

b. The input component of a bicycle is pedaling. ________

c. A chain is used to connect the front gear and the rear gear of a bicycle. ________

d. A front gear with fewer teeth and a rear gear with more teeth are best for biking uphill. ________

2. Match the correct descriptions with each diagram.

front (50 teeth) **and rear** (15 teeth) **front** (20 teeth) **and rear** (35 teeth)	**move slowly** **move fast**	**easy to pedal** **hard to pedal**

Biking on Level Ground

- ____________________
- ____________________
- ____________________

Biking Uphill

- ____________________
- ____________________
- ____________________

4 Gears around Us

There are many machines that use gears all around us. We use different types of gears to make our jobs easier. In this unit, you will learn how different types of gears work and how they change the speed, direction, and motion of moving objects.

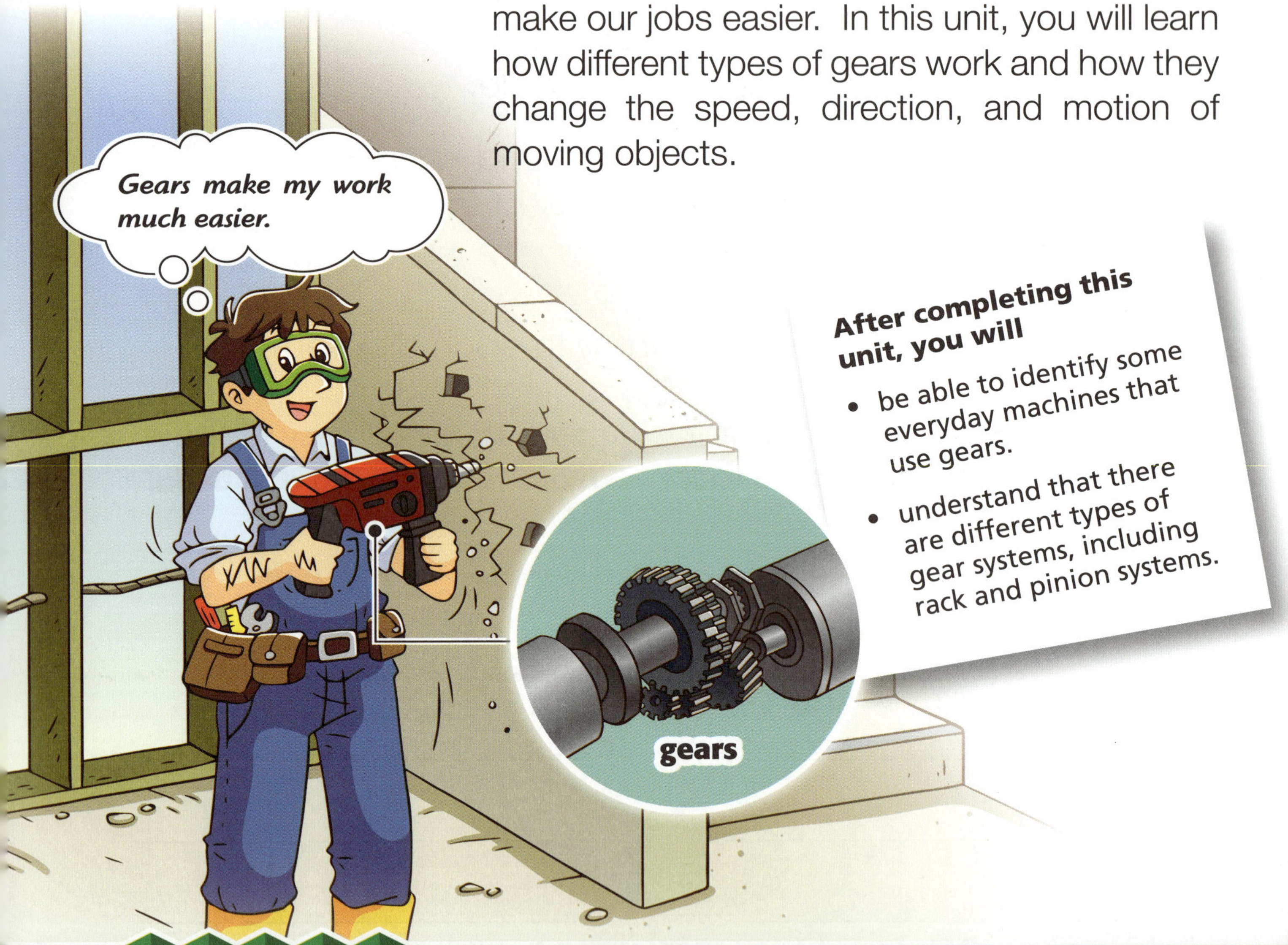

After completing this unit, you will

- be able to identify some everyday machines that use gears.
- understand that there are different types of gear systems, including rack and pinion systems.

Vocabulary

simple machine: a device that changes the direction or magnitude of a force

compound machine: a machine made up of two or more simple machines

Extension

Take a closer look at a can opener and you will see that it is made up of several simple machines. To use a can opener, you squeeze two levers together. This action pushes the wedge into the can. When you turn the handle, the wheel and axle turn the wedge to cut the lid away from the can with the help of a pair of gears.

A. Name the simple machines that are used with gears to make each compound machine.

1.

simple machines used:

____

____

2.

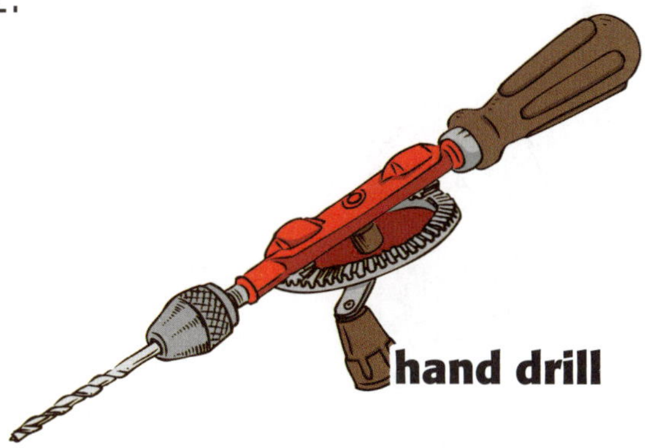

simple machines used:

____

____

____

B. Name the gears. Then fill in the blanks.

bevel gears worm gear idler gear spur gears	one two shafts direction same worm one two

1.

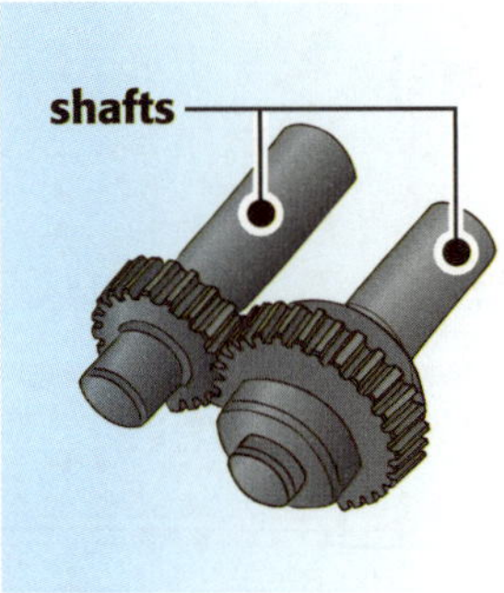

- s__________ g__________
- straight teeth, mounted on parallel __________
- operate in __________ plane

2.

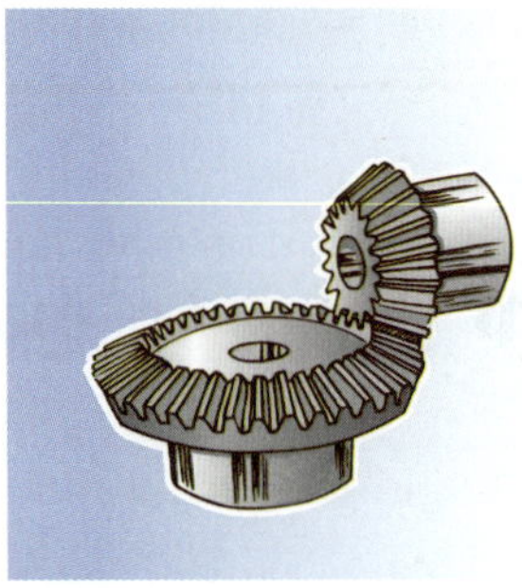

- b__________ g__________
- change the __________ of movement
- operate in __________ planes

3.

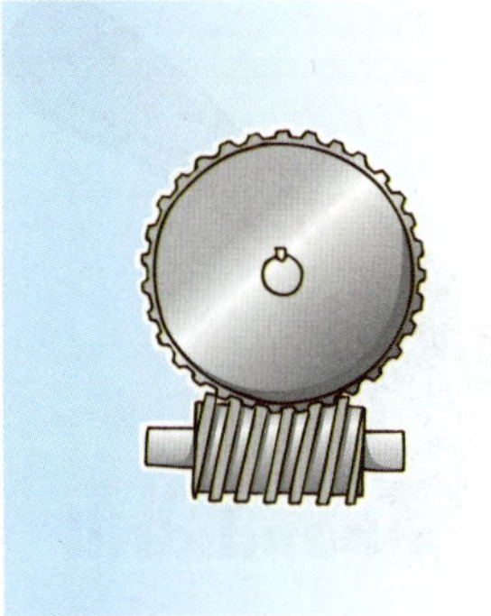

- a w__________ g__________ system
- a combination of a circular gear and a __________ gear
- operates in __________ planes

4.

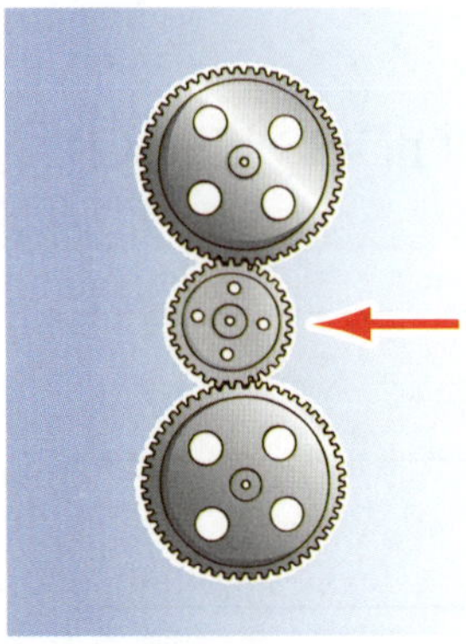

- an i__________ g__________
- used to keep two connected gears rotating in the __________ direction
- operates in __________ plane

C. **Draw arrows to show how the gears turn. Then write and check the correct answers.**

Rack and Pinion System

A single gear, a pinion, meshes with a sliding toothed rack.

1.

The rack moves to the left.

The rack moves to the right.

2. A rack and pinion system converts rotary motion to ______________ motion.
linear/dynamic

3. Go online with the permission from an adult and see which are examples of machines that use a rack and pinion system. Check the circles.

(A) the rear wheel of a bicycle

(B) windshield wipers in cars

(C) a clock pendulum

(D) the pointer in a bathroom scale

(E) the wheel of a wheelbarrow

D. Read Celine's activity sheet. Then answer the questions.

Science and Technology — Name: *Celine Winter*

Build a Gear System

You will need two or more gears.

Objective: to build a gear system of two or more gears to achieve a goal

Fast Fact
Chains can be used to make two gears turn in the same direction.

Plan *My plan is to make a ballet show with two ballerina dolls; each doll will stand on a gear. Turning one of the dolls will make the other doll turn and they will perform a show.*

My Idea

1. In Celine's design, do the ballerina dolls spin

   a. in the same direction? ____________

   b. at the same speed? ____________

2. If Celine wants to have the ballerina dolls turn in the same direction, in which two ways can she do it? Write about each way and draw a diagram with gears to support your ideas.

Way 1

____

____

____

Way 2

____

____

____

3. If Celine wants to have the ballerina dolls turn at different speeds, what can she do? Write about it and draw a diagram.

____

____

____

____

____

5 Pulleys Everywhere

We use pulleys every day and pulleys can be found everywhere. In this unit, you will identify pulleys that are used in our daily lives and understand how a pulley works and how to use one.

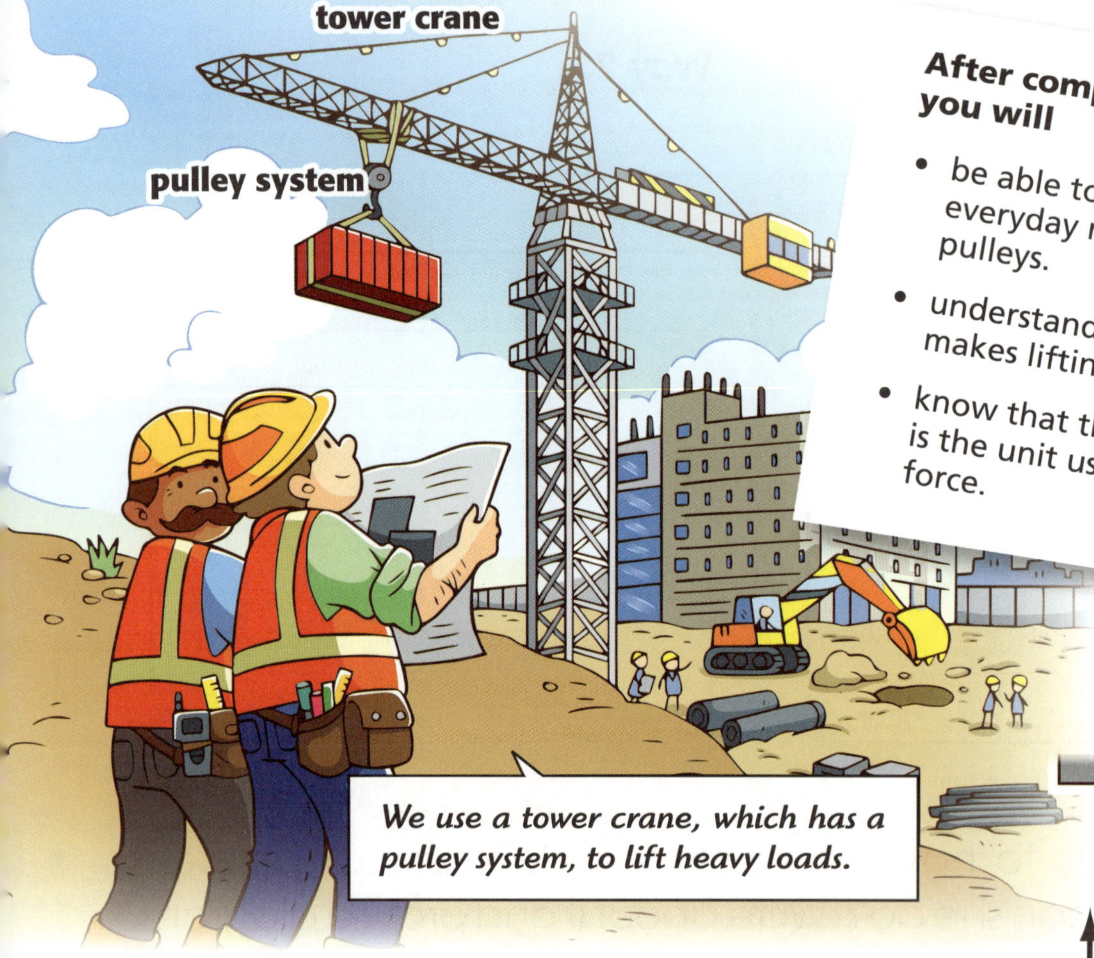

After completing this unit, you will

- be able to identify many everyday machines that use pulleys.
- understand why a pulley makes lifting a load easier.
- know that the newton (N) is the unit used to measure force.

Vocabulary

pulley: a simple machine consisting of a grooved wheel and a rope that runs over the wheel

load: a weight that is supported or lifted

Extension

Pulleys are important simple machines that are widely used in our daily lives. In the Middle Ages, people used pulleys to lift heavy stone blocks to build the walls of castles.

Cranes, like the one shown in the picture, were used to build large, stone buildings in the Middle Ages. The crane was powered by men running inside the two huge wheels.

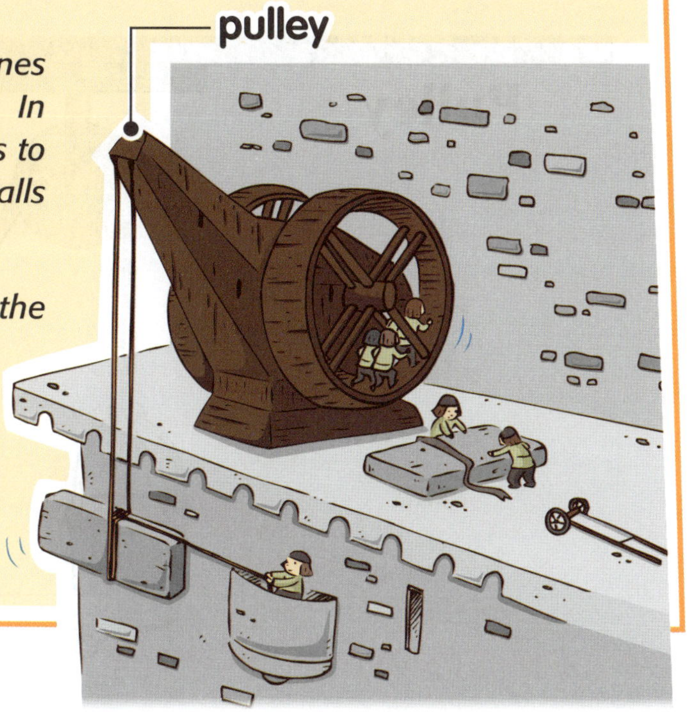

A. Go online with an adult's permission and see which are examples of pulleys found at home. Check the circles.

Ⓐ

Ⓑ

Ⓒ garage door

Ⓓ eggbeater

Ⓔ portable vacuum cleaner

Ⓕ retractable clothesline

B. Trace the arrows to show the movement. Then label the diagram.

1.

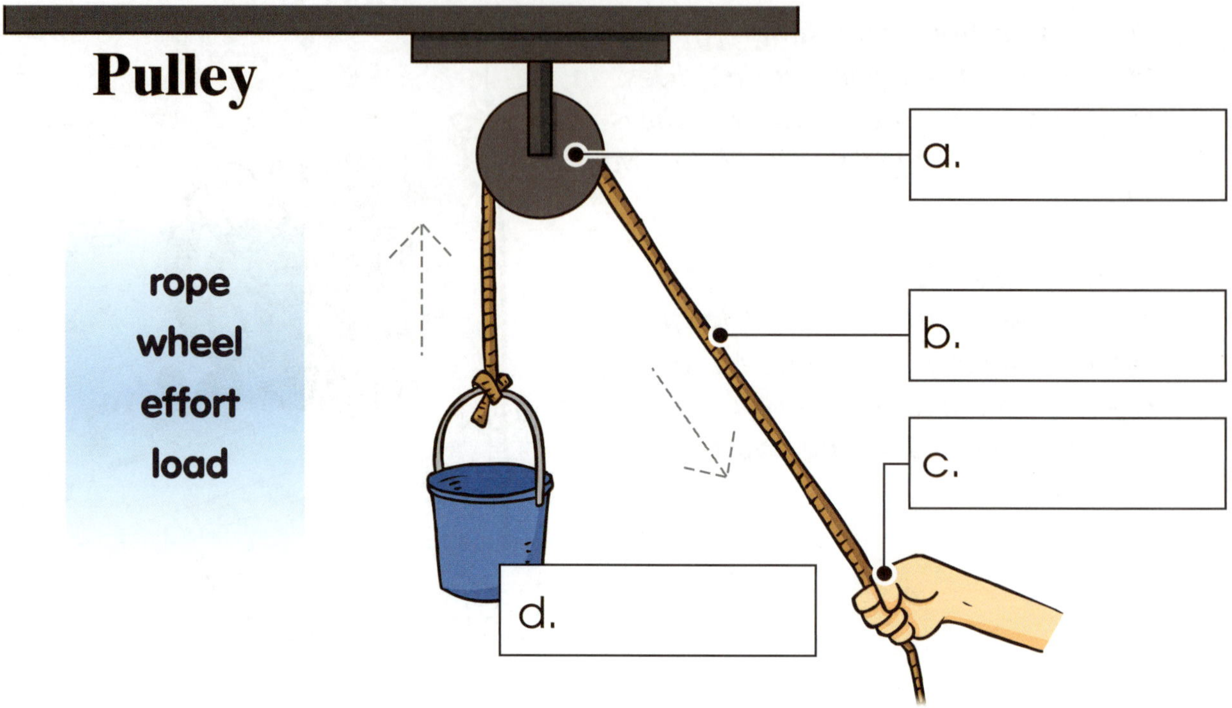

2. When you pull down on the rope, the load will go **up / down** .

C. Ted did experiments on lifting weights with and without the help of a pulley. Look at his records. Then answer the questions.

Force Needed to Lift a Weight

Weight	Without a Pulley	With a Pulley
10 N*	10 N	10 N
30 N	30 N	30 N
50 N	50 N	50 N

*N is the abbreviation for the newton, the unit for measuring force.

This device is used to measure force.

1. How much force is needed to lift a weight of 50 N

   a. without using a pulley? ____________

   b. with a pulley? ____________

2. Predict how much force is needed to lift a weight of 80 N

   a. without using a pulley. ____________

   b. with a pulley. ____________

3. The amount of force needed to lift a load in both cases is ____________ (the same/different), but you may find that it is ____________ (easier/harder) to pull down than it is to pull up.

4. A pulley lets you use your ____________ (weight/height) to lift a load.

5. *I use a pulley to make it easier to lift a bucket of water from the well. Show how this can be done by drawing it.*

D. Read the passage. Then answer the questions.

Everyday Pulleys

The uses of pulleys are endless. In **recreation**, pulleys are used to keep rock climbers safe in indoor gyms. They are essential parts in many weight-lifting exercise machines. Sailboats use many fixed and movable pulleys to raise, lower, and change the position of sails. In **construction**, pulleys are used in cranes, which move construction materials vertically and horizontally. Pulleys are important in **shipping** as well. Heavy loads are lifted and lowered using cranes and forklifts, both of which use pulleys. Pulleys are also used in **building maintenance** to lift and lower hanging scaffolding, which provides a moving platform for workers who paint or repair the exteriors of tall buildings or wash windows. At **home**, pulleys are used in garage doors, window blinds, and clotheslines. Some **restaurants** have small elevators called dumbwaiters that use a pulley system to move food from the kitchen to the dining floors.

1. Give an example of how pulleys are used in each area mentioned in the passage.

Area	Machines with Pulleys (function)
• in buildings	elevators – allow easy access to all floors
• ____________	____________
• ____________	____________
• ____________	____________
• ____________	____________
• ____________	____________
• ____________	____________

2. Look at the diagram of an elevator.

Elevator

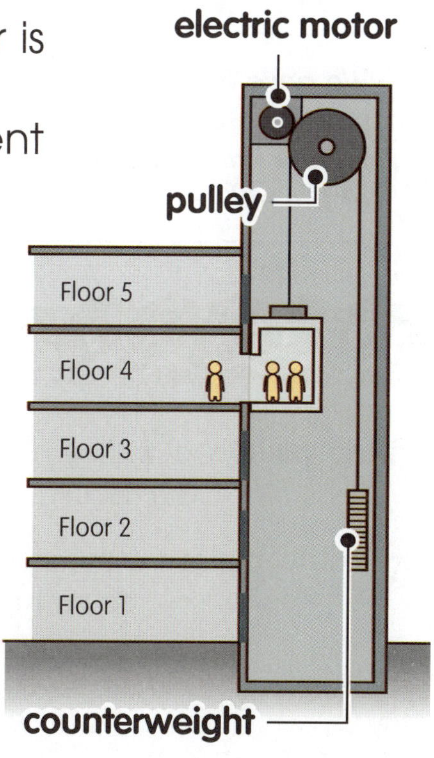

a. The upward movement of the elevator is linked to the ____________ (upward/downward) movement of a counterweight.

b. Mr. Winter is on the fourth floor. If he wants to go to the first floor, how should the counterweight move?

____

6 Pulley Power

A single fixed pulley can help us lift and lower loads by changing the direction of our force. We can also connect movable pulleys in order to use less force to lift a load. In this unit, you will see how movable pulleys divide the weight of a load, and how the number of pulleys in a system can affect the force required to lift a load.

After completing this unit, you will

- understand the difference between a single pulley and a pulley system.
- know what a movable pulley is.
- understand the advantages of pulley systems.

Vocabulary

fixed pulley: a pulley attached to a fixed structure

movable pulley: a pulley attached to the load being lifted

Extension

Pulleys are widely used, from window blinds in our homes to cranes on construction sites. Did you know that we also use pulleys in hospitals to help patients with broken bones?

A pulley system helps stretch the tight muscles around a broken bone but keeps the broken bone in place so that it will heal properly.

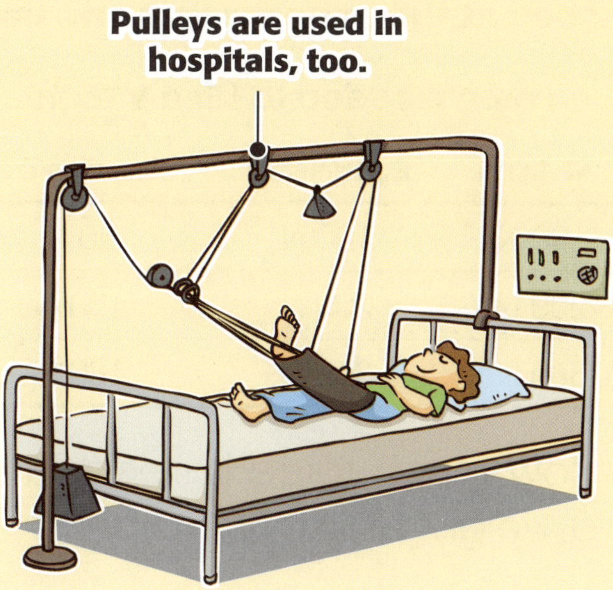

A. Write a short paragraph to describe how a flagpole works.

How a Pulley Makes a Flagpole Work

____

____

____

____

____

____

____

B. Look at the experiments and the records. Answer the questions.

Force Needed to Lift a Weight

Weight	Experiment 1	Experiment 2
100 N	100 N	50 N
200 N	200 N	100 N
360 N	360 N	180 N

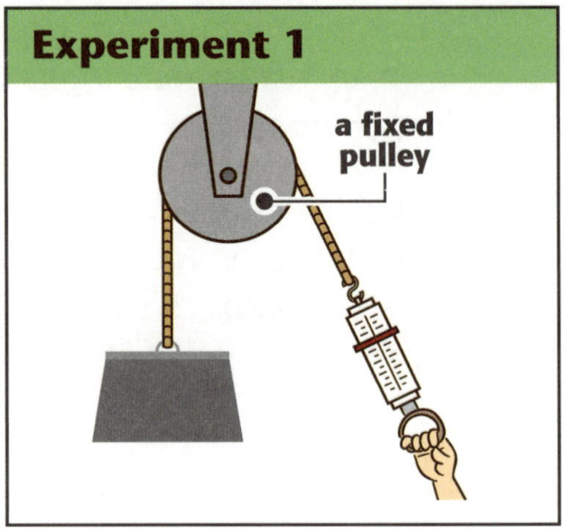

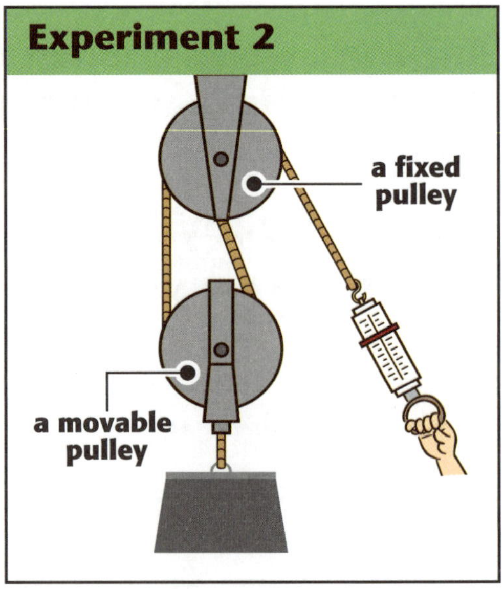

1. How much force is needed to lift a weight of 200 N

   a. with one pulley in Experiment 1? ____________

   b. with two pulleys in Experiment 2? ____________

2. Predict how much force is needed to lift a weight of 420 N

   a. with one pulley in Experiment 1. ____________

   b. with two pulleys in Experiment 2. ____________

3. A system with a fixed pulley and a movable pulley requires ________________ (none of/half) the amount of effort needed to lift a load with one fixed pulley.

4. What happens when the number of movable pulleys in a system is increased?

   ____

C. Look at the experiments. Complete the records. Then answer the questions.

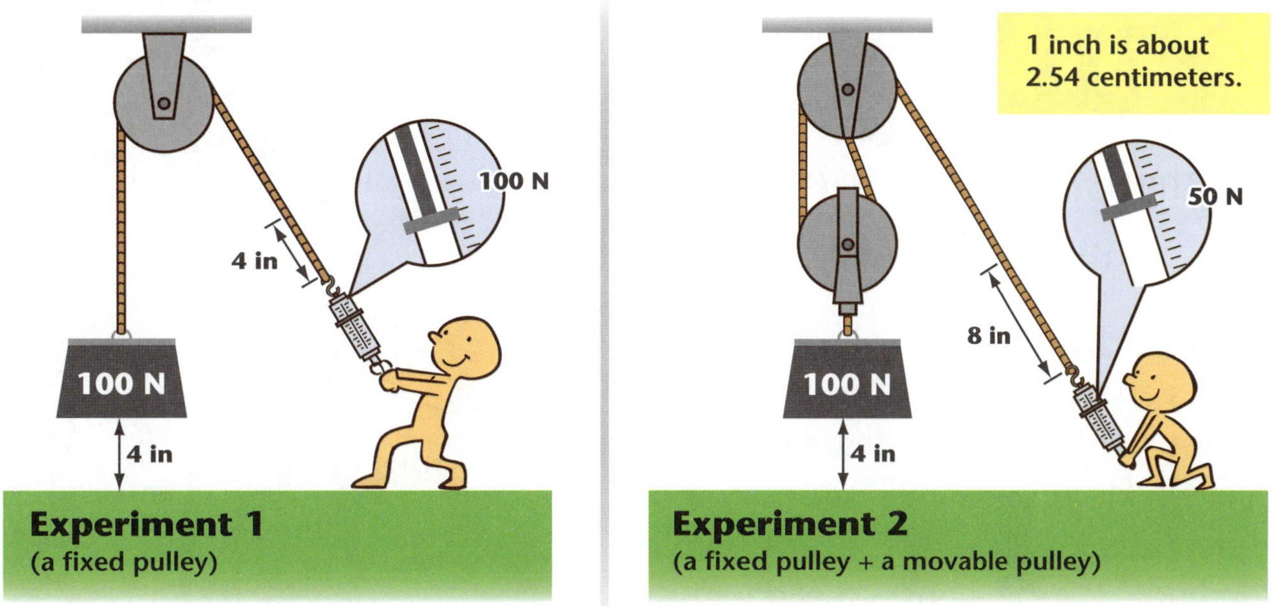

1. Lifting a Weight of 100 N 4 inches High

	Force Needed	Distance of Rope Pulled
Experiment 1		
Experiment 2		

2. The experiments show that the force is cut in ________ (half/a second) when a movable pulley is added, but the distance the rope must be pulled has ________ (tripled/doubled).

3. How does the distance over which the force is exerted change when the number of movable pulleys in a system is increased?

____

D. Read the passage. Then answer the questions.

Pulleys and the Canal Ring Houses in Amsterdam

In Amsterdam, a canal city in Europe, pulleys adorn the tops of many houses. Houses built along Amsterdam's many canals in the 1600s are tall and narrow to protect the possessions inside them from flooding. Narrow houses mean narrow doorways and narrow, steep staircases, making it challenging to move large items within a house. Then how do people move their belongings from one floor to another? With pulleys! At the top of these houses is a hoist beam. A pulley is either attached to this beam, or the hoist beam leads to a pulley system in the attic. This way, furniture can be moved from floor to floor outside the house. To ensure that bigger items do not hit the exterior walls while being lifted or lowered, many houses are built tilted outward to provide space between the house and the item.

1. Check the building that might be found in Amsterdam.

2. Draw pictures to show how a couch is moved to the second floor.

With a Fixed Pulley

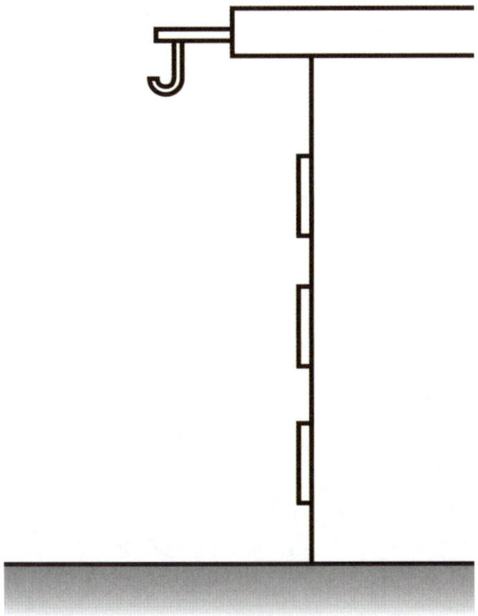

With a Fixed Pulley and a Movable Pulley

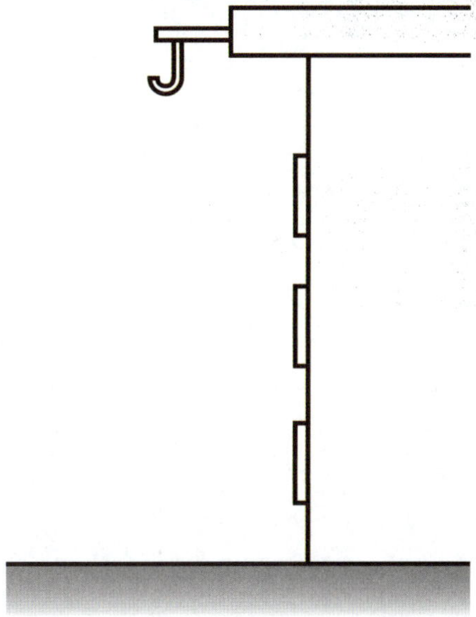

3. If the couch weighs 1,000 N, how much force is needed to lift it

a. with a fixed pulley? ____________

b. with a fixed pulley and a movable pulley? ____________

POWERFUL PULLEYS

understanding how pulleys work and how they make lifting easier

Pulleys are used in zip lines.

Pulleys are all around us. From window blinds at homes to cranes on construction sites, pulleys are simple machines that we often use to make lifting easier. When you pull the strings of the window blinds down, the blinds go up. When it comes to putting a roof on a house, construction workers will use the pull-down force in the crane to lift the roof and place it on the house. Try this experiment to see how much easier it is to do work with pulleys.

What you need:

a big plastic jug with a handle

water

string

a spool

a pencil

Difficulty: ●●●○○

Time needed:
30 minutes

This experiment will help you understand how a pulley makes work easier.

What to do:

1. Insert the pencil into the spool.
2. Tie a string on one end of the pencil. Let the string go around a rod twice and tie the other end of the pencil to make a pulley. Make sure that the pulley is secured tightly in a balanced position.
3. Fill the jug with some water. Tie the handle to a string that is 6.5 ft (about 2 m) long.
4. Leave the jug on the floor. Lift the jug using the string.
5. Leave the jug on the floor right below the pulley.
6. Bring the string over the spool.
7. Pull the string down until the jug is off the floor. How much effort was required this time?

WHAT *just* happened?

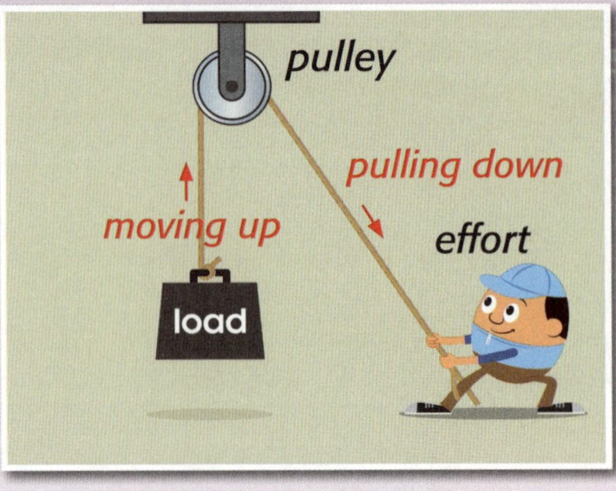

You should have noticed that it was easier to lift the jug with the help of the pulley. Pulleys are incredible simple machines that help us do work more easily by changing the direction of the force we apply.

In the experiment, the pulley allowed you to pull down to lift the jug, meaning that you could take advantage of gravity to help lift it. Gravity is the force that pulls things downward toward the ground. When you pulled the string down, the pulley redirected that force and lifted the jug.

But that's not all! The pulley also allowed you to use your own body weight to help lift the jug. When you pulled down on the rope, your body weight added to the pull to lift the jug. With the pulley, you can use the force of gravity exerted on you to accomplish the task with less effort.

Pulleys are used in many different places, like on cranes to lift heavy loads or in well systems to bring up buckets of water from deep underground. Pulleys are simple yet powerful machines that help us in our daily lives!

STEM INQUIRY

- Go on a pulley scavenger hunt. How many pulleys can you find in your home?
- What are some jobs that a pulley can make easier?
- By lifting the jug of water, what force are you trying to overcome?
- Where did friction occur in this experiment?

- What will happen if two pulleys are used to lift the load? Design a two-pulley system and compare the efforts needed to lift the water jug.

- Weigh the jug of water. How much weight can you lift with the pulley?
- How far did you have to pull the string to lift the jug 6 in (about 15 cm)?

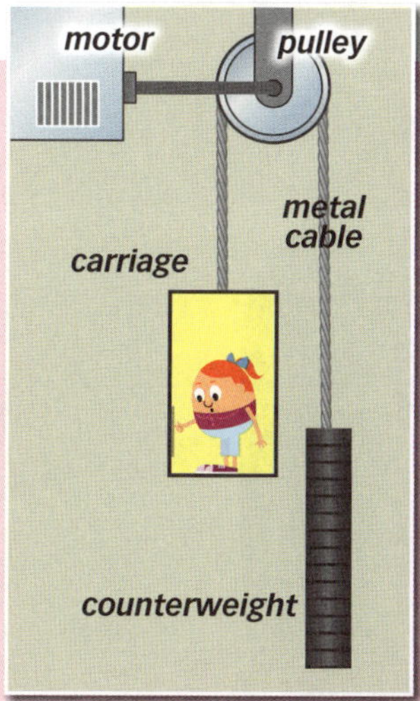

Fun to know

Pulleys in Elevators

Pulleys are commonly used in elevators. In an elevator, the carriage and the counterweight, which balances the weight of the carriage, are attached to the two ends of a strong metal cable. A pulley with grooves holds the cable tightly. The pulley is connected to a motor so that when you push a button inside the carriage, the motor will turn the pulley, moving you up and down.

A TEAM OF PULLEYS

understanding how several pulleys work together to do lifting work

When we put a grooved wheel on a fixed axle and have a rope running on the groove, we create a great lifting machine – a pulley. We can do our lifting work more easily with the help of pulleys. If there are more pulleys in a design, will our lifting work be even easier? Try this experiment to see how to create a lifting machine with a fixed pulley and a movable pulley to do work for us.

What you need:

a pencil

2 spools

string

a lunch bag with some fruits

a key ring

Difficulty: ●●●○○

Time needed: 1 hour

In this experiment, you will construct your own pulley system.

What to do:

Setup A

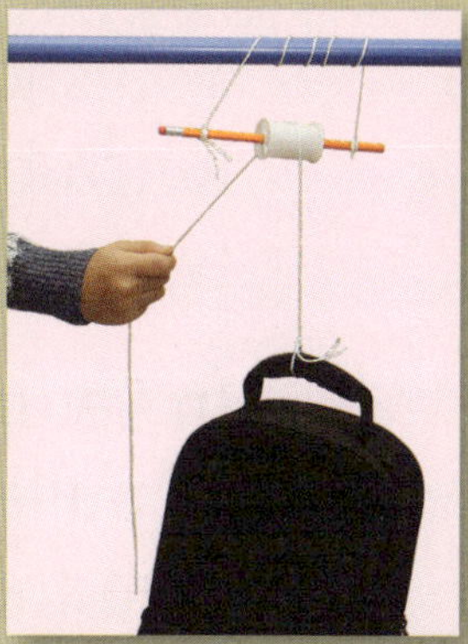

1. Bring a piece of string over a rod twice to set up the structure as shown. Balance the structure.
2. Tie one end of another piece of string to the lunch bag.
3. Pull the string over the spool to lift the lunch bag. Remember how hard you had to pull it.

Setup B

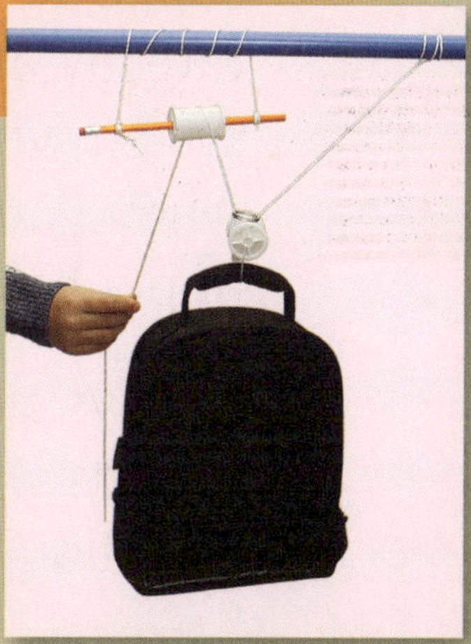

1. Keep the structure you used in Setup A.
2. Thread a piece of string through a spool and tie both ends to the lunch bag.
3. Run a string around the spool and have both ends of the string go through the key ring.
4. Tie one end of the string to the rod.
5. Bring the other end of the string over the spool in the structure built in Setup A.
6. Pull the string to lift the lunch bag. How hard did you have to pull it this time?

WHAT *just* happened?

You should have noticed that it was easier to lift the lunch bag in Setup B. This is because there were two pulleys working together.

In Setup B, there were two types of pulleys. The spool hung up with the pencil acted as a fixed pulley and the spool attached to the lunch bag was a movable pulley. The fixed pulley stayed in place, while the movable pulley could move up and down.

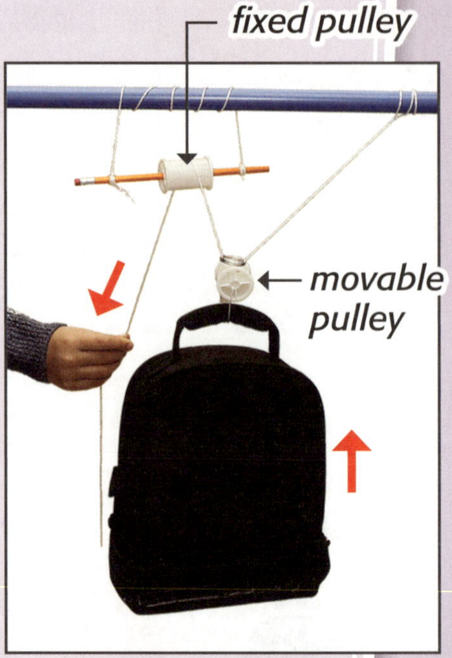

The lunch bag with the movable pulley attached was already supported by the string that was directly attached to the rod in the system you built. Because of this arrangement, when you pulled the string down, you only had to apply half the effort to raise the lunch bag.

Pulleys are fantastic tools that allow us to lift heavy objects with less effort, not only by changing the direction of the force but also by sharing the load.

- Why was the key ring important in the experiment?
- Name as many differences between fixed pulleys and movable pulleys as you can.

- How does the weight of movable pulleys affect the efficiency of a pulley system? Can you install a movable pulley that has the same weight as the load you want to lift? Why or why not?
- Does the weight of fixed pulleys affect the efficiency of a pulley system?

- How far do you have to pull the string to lift the lunch bag 6 in (about 15 cm) in Setup A? What about in Setup B? Find the relationship between the distance you pulled the string and the height the lunch bag was lifted by repeating the experiment. Record your measurements in a chart like the one below.

Distance Pulled vs. Lifted Height

Distance You Pulled the String	Height the Lunch Bag Was Lifted	
	Setup A	Setup B

Fun to know

Window Cleaning

Cleaning windows on skyscrapers can be a real challenge. Other than using safety belts and scaffolds, the use of pulleys is also very common. Thanks to the multiple pulley systems, cleaners can go up and down easily by pulling the ropes.

TEETH ON GEARS
understanding how gears work

Gears are everywhere. We find them in clocks, on bicycles, in cars, and in many machines. They are usually circular and have teeth all around them. Gears are awesome tools that transfer motion.

What you need:

thick cardboard

glue

scissors

2 pins

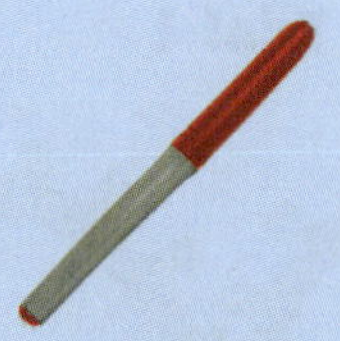
a marker

2 plastic lids

Difficulty: ●●●○○

Time needed: 1 hour

In this experiment, you will build your own gears and see how they work.

What to do:

1.

Cut two thin and long strips of cardboard.

2.
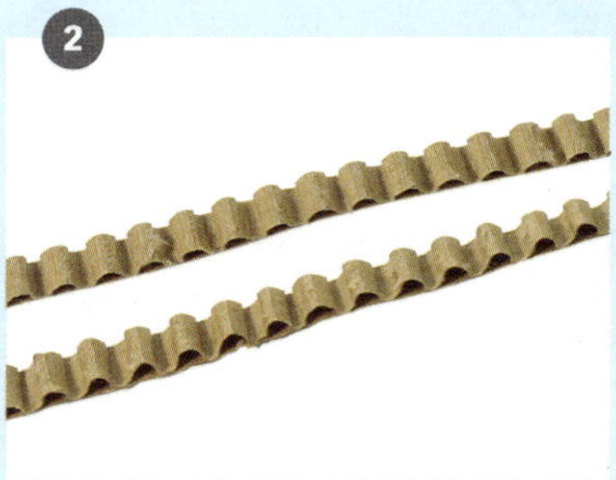
Peel off one side of each strip carefully to avoid breaking the zigzag structure.

3.

Glue the flat side of the strips to the plastic lids to make two "gears."

4.
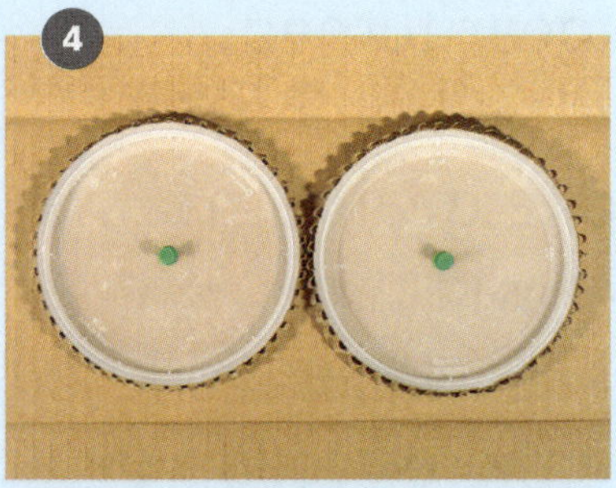
Pin the centers of the lids with the pins to the cardboard.

5.

Draw a line on each lid and position it vertically.

6.

Turn the gears and record your observations in the chart on the next page.

My Record

Draw an arrow to show how the other gear turned in each pair.

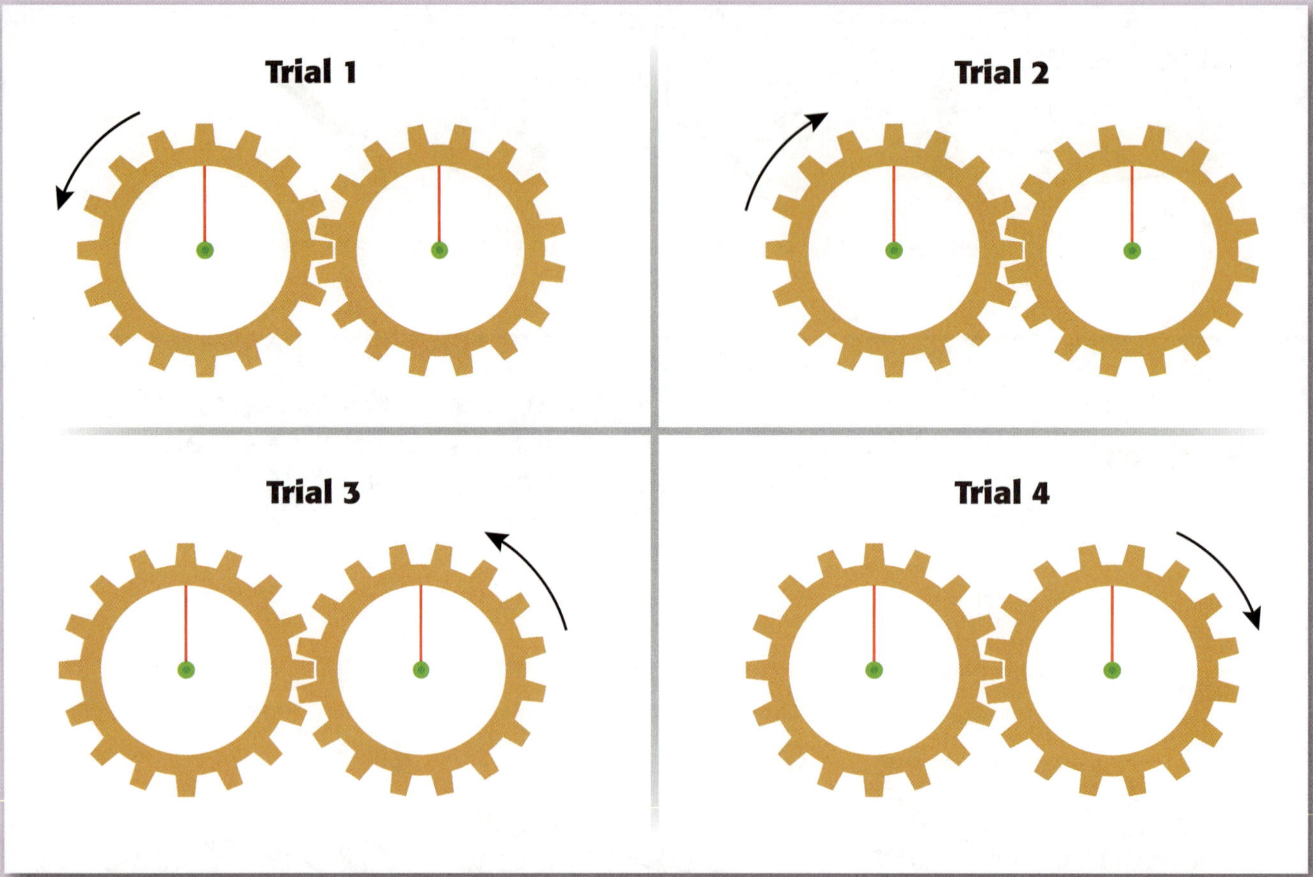

WHAT *just* happened?

In the experiment, when you turned one gear, the other gear turned too. This happened because the teeth of the gears were in contact. So when one gear turned, its teeth caused the other gear to turn with it but in the opposite direction. It means that when one gear turns clockwise, the other will turn counterclockwise. Gears can work together to change the direction of motion.

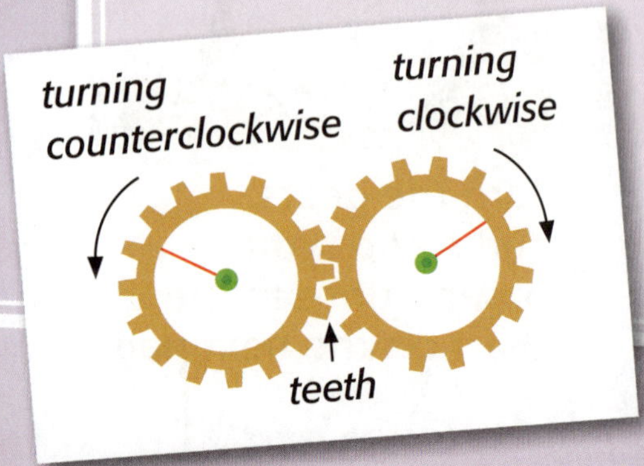

STEM INQUIRY

- Which simple machines make up a gear?
- Can a gear work alone?

- Have you wondered how clocks work? Typically, there are at least three gears in a clock. You can investigate the gears by yourself if you could find an old broken analog clock or watch at home, or research online with the permission from an adult to learn about this mechanism.

- Design a creative gear system that transmits power to different directions. Use your imagination to make it fun. Try ideas like a puppet, carousel, and teacup ride.

- Try the experiment with two plastic lids of different sizes. Which size of the gears turns faster? For every turn of the big gear, how many turns do the small gear make? Make a chart like the one below to record your results. What do you find?

Big Gear vs. Small Gear

	Big Gear	Small Gear
Number of Turns		

Fun to know

Gear Train

A gear train is a sequence of two or more gears. Each gear in a train causes the next gear to move in the opposite direction. For this reason, it is common to use an odd number of gears in a gear train because the motion can be transferred in the same direction.

TWIST AND TURN!

understanding how screws work

Have you ever tightened wooden cabinets with screws and a screwdriver? If so, can you describe the motion involved? As a screw turns, it goes into the wood pieces to hold them together. Screws are not only used to fasten things, however. They can also be found in many things such as bottle caps and faucets.

STEM Note

Most screws require matching screwdrivers to tighten them and carry out their functions. Below are two common screw heads.

- Phillips-head
- flat-head

What you need:

- a cardboard sheet
- a water bottle
- a bowl
- scissors
- a cardboard tube
- gumballs
- tape
- a pencil

Difficulty:
●●●●○

Time needed:
1 hour

In this experiment, you will see how screws convert rotational motion into linear motion.

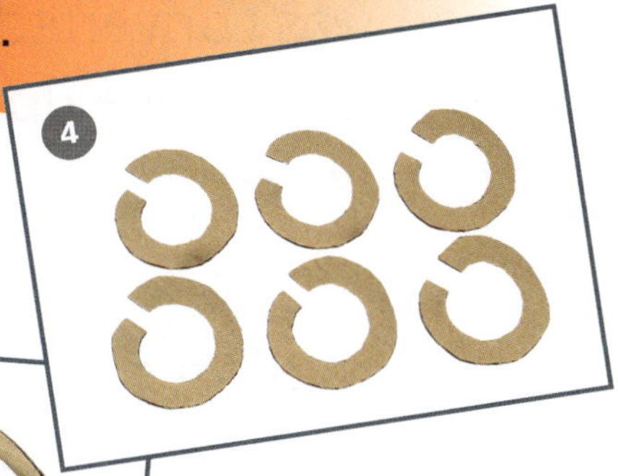

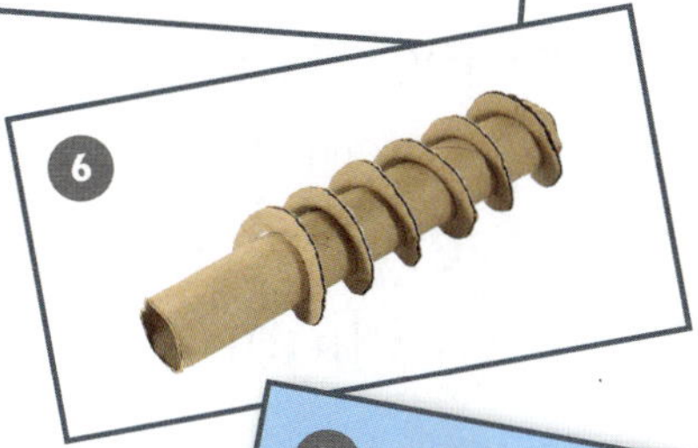

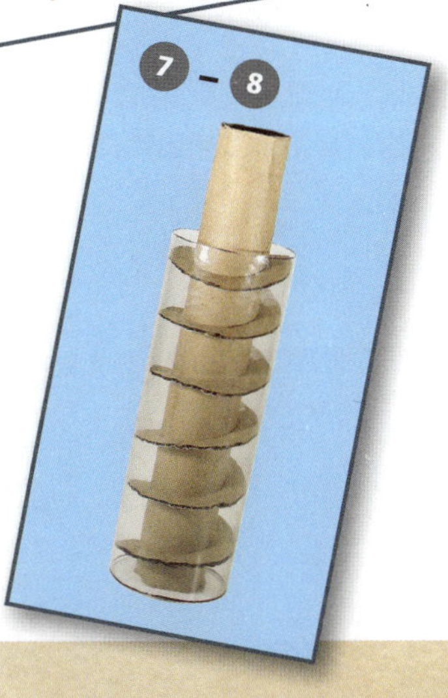

What to do:

1. Trace the water bottle on the cardboard sheet to get six circles. Cut out the circles.
2. Draw a line from the center of each circle to its edge.
3. Trace the cardboard tube in the center of each circle.
4. Cut along the line. Then cut out the small circles to get six rings with slits.
5. Tape the rings together to make a spiral.
6. Wrap the spiral around the tube. Secure it with tape.
7. Cut off the top and bottom of the water bottle.
8. Put the spiral in the bottle.
9. Insert the bottle into a bowl filled with gumballs at an angle.
10. Hold the bottle and turn the tube slowly and observe. What happened to the gumballs?

WHAT just happened?

As the tube was turned in one direction, the gumballs started moving up along the spiral and eventually came out from the top of the tube. This experiment demonstrated how a screw, which is a simple machine, works.

By turning the tube, you created rotational motion, which is the movement of an object when it turns around a fixed point, like the motion of twisting the lid off a jar or turning a doorknob. The spiral inside the tube acted as a screw and provided a slope for the gumballs to move upward. When you turned the tube, the rotational motion was converted into linear motion, making the gumballs move up in a straight line, and eventually, they came out from the top of the tube.

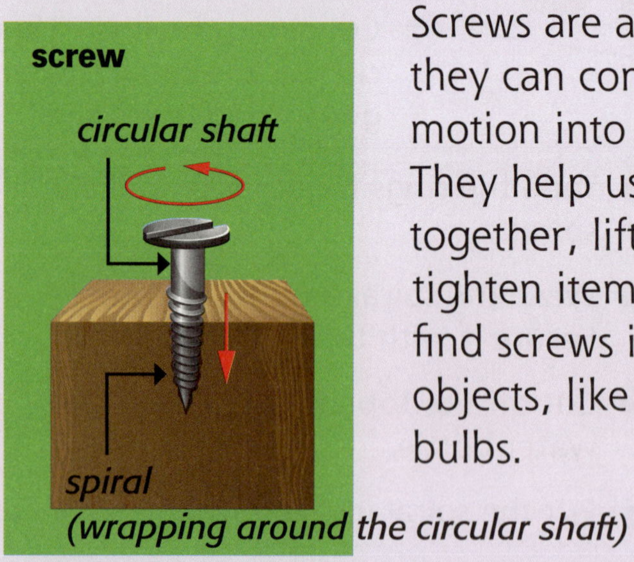

Screws are amazing because they can convert rotational motion into linear motion. They help us fasten things together, lift heavy objects, or tighten items securely. You can find screws in many everyday objects, like drill bits and light bulbs.

STEM INQUIRY

- What other simple machine is a screw made of?
- Screws and nails can be used to hold two pieces of wood together. How is a screw designed differently from a nail?

- An Archimedes' screw was originally designed to get rid of water on a boat. Go online with the permission from an adult to find information about how an Archimedes' screw works.

- With the help of an adult, find a piece of wood, a nail, and a screw. Try to put the nail into the wood using your hand. Then try to put the screw into the piece of wood. Which one was easier to put into the wood?

- A figure has rotational symmetry if it fits on itself within a complete rotation. Draw a figure that has rotational symmetry and fits on itself four times within a complete rotation.

e.g.

This figure fits on itself three times within a complete rotation.

Fun to know

Screwing into Ice

Ice fishing is a fun winter activity. To create a hole in the ice for fishing, many ice fishermen use a hand auger. The hand auger makes drilling holes into the ice a lot easier as all they need to do is twist and turn.

Section 3

Matter and Energy

1 Light around Us

Light is a form of energy that is all around us. In this unit, you will see that there are natural and artificial light sources and that some objects emit light while others reflect it. You will also see that light travels in straight lines.

After completing this unit, you will

- know that light sources can be natural or artificial.
- know that some objects emit light and others reflect it.
- know that light travels in straight lines.

Vocabulary

natural light: light produced by nature such as sunlight

artificial light: light produced by humans; does not occur naturally

emit: to give off (light)

reflect: to throw back (light) from a surface

artificial light

Extension

Light is all around us, but we cannot hear or feel it. We become aware of it when it reaches our eyes. Without light, we cannot see anything at all! The sun is our main source of light. Its light is very strong and it can reach us even when it is very cloudy. It is so strong that we should never look directly at it, as it could damage our eyes.

A. Fill in the blanks. Then sort the pictures of light sources and give one more example for each.

Light Sources natural artificial

- Light that occurs in nature is

  ____________ light.

  e.g. ( ) ; ____________

- Light that is created by people and does not occur naturally is

  ____________ light.

  e.g. ( ) ; ____________

B. Fill in the blanks with the words "emit" or "reflect." Then sort the objects and answer the question.

What Emits or Reflects Light?

Most things, such as rocks, pencils, and mirrors, do not 1. ____________ their own light; we see them because light bounces off them. They 2. ____________ light. Some things reflect light better than others. Things that 3. ____________ light are our light sources.

Objects That

- emit light:

  4. ____________

- reflect light:

  5. ____________

6. Which objects shown in the picture are safety reflectors? How do they keep people safe?

____

____

C. **Fill in the blanks with the given words. Then check the correct picture in each pair to show how light travels.**

reflected **straight** **direction**

Light travels in 1. ______________ lines. It always travels like this unless it meets something that makes it change 2. ______________ . Once the light hits an object and it changes its direction, we can see the object because the light is 3. ______________ into our eyes. Since light has this property, we are not able to see around a bend in the road.

4.

5.

6.

2 Light: Reflection and Refraction

We see because of light. In this unit, you will learn about two special properties of light, reflection and refraction, and recognize that reflection and refraction are important in our daily lives.

After completing this unit, you will

- know what reflection and refraction of light are.
- understand why we see a rainbow.
- understand how we see colors.

Vocabulary

reflection: the occurrence of light bouncing off an object

refraction: the occurrence of light bending or changing its angle as it passes from one material to another

absorb: to take in (light)

Extension

Pools, lakes, and rivers often appear less deep than they really are because water acts just like a magnifying lens, bending light to make it seem like the bottom of these bodies of water are nearer to us than they truly are. Next time you go swimming, try picking up an object from under the water. You might find that it is deeper than you think.

A. Fill in the blanks with "reflection" or "refraction." Then draw lines to match the pictures with the correct descriptions.

Properties of Light

- When light hits an object and bounces off, it creates a ________________ .

- Light travels in a straight line, but when it passes through another medium such as water, it may bend and change direction. This is called ________________ .

B. Fill in the blanks with the given words. Then color the rainbow.

red	white	direction	refraction	yellow	green
blue	indigo	violet	raindrop	orange	

Since sunlight appears to have no colors, we call it 1. ______________ light, but it is really made up of all the colors of the rainbow: 2. ______________ , 3. ______________ , 4. ______________ , 5. ______________ , 6. ______________ , 7. ______________ , and 8. ______________ . When white light meets a 9. ______________ , it changes 10. ______________ . This change of direction is called 11. ______________ . When the colors in the light are refracted and separated, a beautiful rainbow is formed.

An Example of Refraction

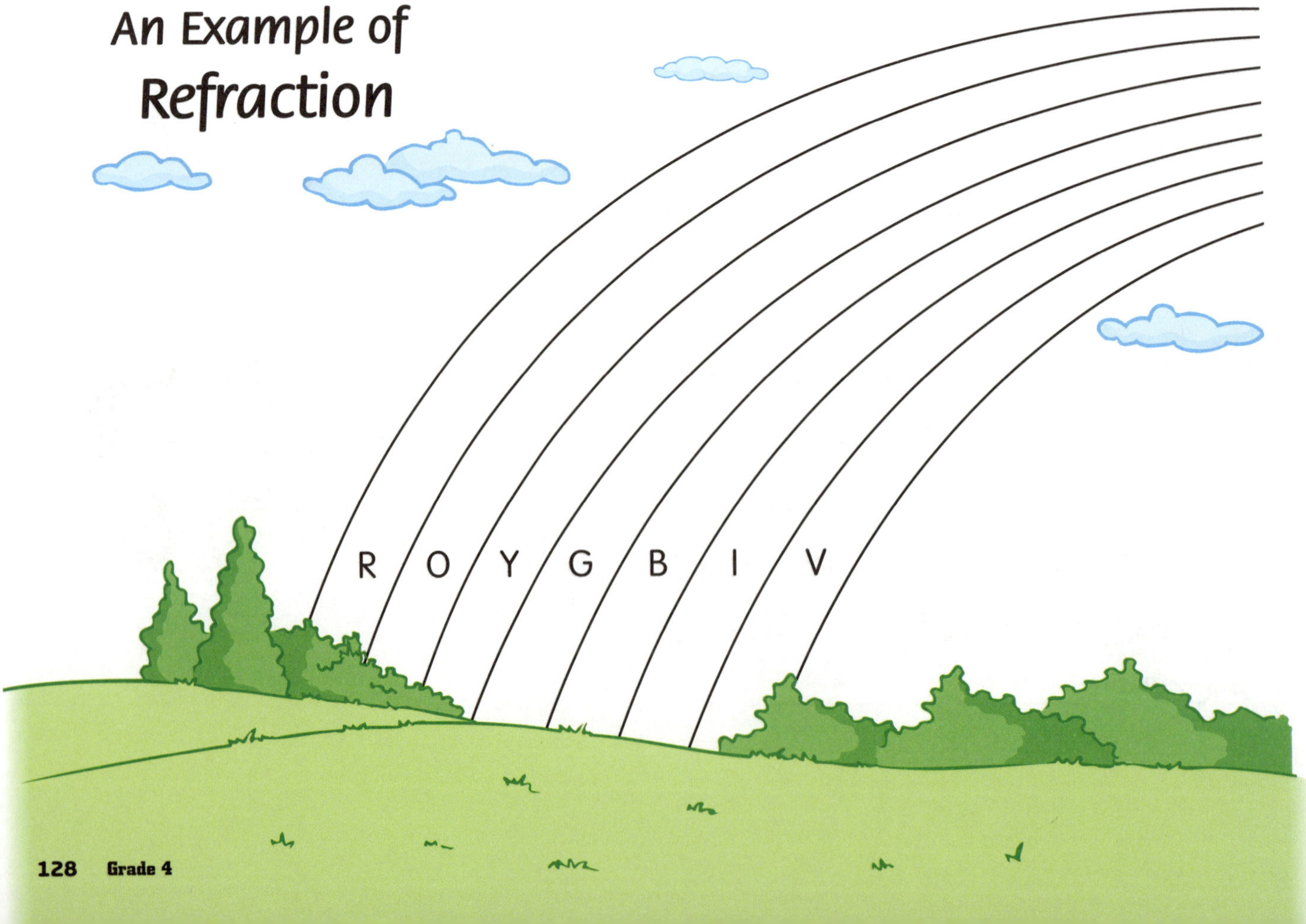

C. **Fill in the blanks to complete the descriptions. Then answer the question.**

How Do We See Colors?

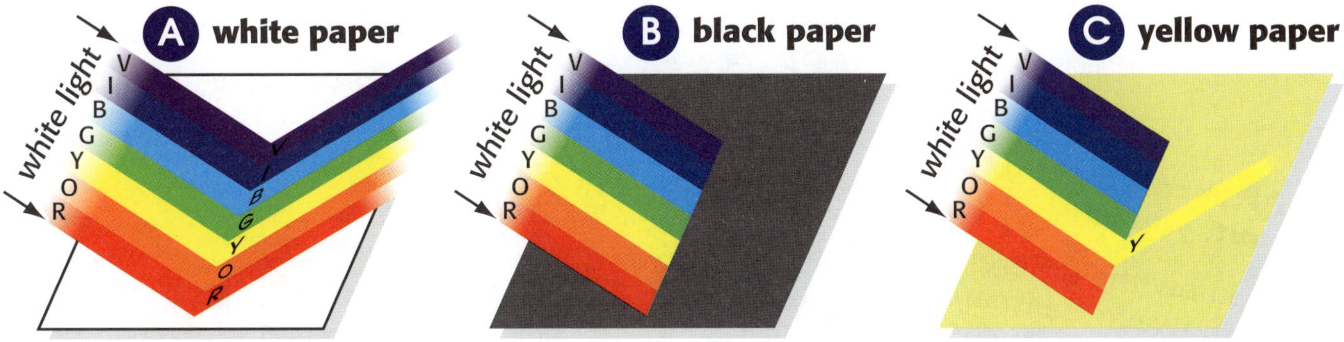

(A) When sunlight shines on a white surface, we see ____________ (white/black) because the surface ____________ (reflects/absorbs) all the colors.

(B) When sunlight shines on a black surface, we see ____________ (white/black) because all the colors have been taken in or ____________ (reflected/absorbed) .

(C) When sunlight shines on a yellow surface, we see ____________ (yellow/red) because all the colors except yellow have been ____________ (reflected/absorbed) by the surface.

What makes a green frog green?

____

____

3 Light: Transparency

Light can pass through some materials but not others. In this unit, you will see what some of these materials are. You will also see how shadows are formed.

After completing this unit, you will

- know the difference between transparent, translucent, and opaque materials and understand why they are used.
- understand how a shadow is formed.

Vocabulary

transparent: allowing light to pass through easily; can be seen through clearly

translucent: allowing only some light to pass through; cannot be seen through clearly

opaque: allowing no light to pass through; cannot be seen through

Extension

Have you ever paid attention to your shadow? When you stand outdoors in the sunlight, light cannot pass through your body. Some light is reflected and some is absorbed by your body. Therefore, there is an area on the ground that light does not reach. This is your shadow.

The size of your shadow is not fixed. Do you know how to make it shrink or grow?

A. Color each rectangle with the specified color. Then fill in the blanks.

opaque transparent translucent

1. ______________ material:
   - Light passes through it, allowing objects to be seen clearly.

2. ______________ material:
   - Some light passes through it, causing objects to be seen less clearly.

3. ______________ material:
   - No light passes through it, preventing objects from being seen.

B. Identify the material each object is made of and decide which type of material each person needs.

Material

- Transparent
- Translucent
- Opaque

- Sam does not want people to touch his sculpture, but he wants them to be able to see it.
- Emma does not want her father to see the gift she has made him.
- Sasha wants a window on her door, but she still wants to have some privacy.

C. Write a situation when it would be best to use each type of material.

Transparent: ______________________________

Translucent: ______________________________

Opaque: ______________________________

D. Fill in the blanks with the given words. Then check the correct shadows and cross out the incorrect one.

straight　　opaque　　length　　shadow

Light travels in 1. ____________ lines. When light cannot pass through an object, the object casts a 2. ____________ . Therefore, 3. ____________ objects cast shadows. The 4. ____________ , size, and position of a shadow depend on where the light is coming from in relation to an object.

5.

6.

7.

4 What Is Sound?

A sound is made when something vibrates. In this unit, you will learn about how vibrations cause sounds and how sounds travel. You will also learn about how a sound's pitch is related to vibration.

After completing this unit, you will

- know what sound is.
- know how sound travels.
- know what pitch is.

Vocabulary

vibration: a quick, back-and-forth motion

pitch: the lowness or highness of a sound

Extension

In different environments, we can hear different sounds. Go to some different places and make a chart to record the sounds that you hear. Then describe the loudness of the sounds and write about how the sounds make you feel. Do some sounds make you feel nervous, energetic, calm, or happy?

Stadium – sounds that I can hear
1. **screaming**: loud, makes me excited
2. **clapping**: not loud, makes me happy

A. Look at the pictures. Then fill in the blanks with the given words.

vibrates
vibrate
sound
vibrating

The Cause of Sound: Vibration

Hold one end of a ruler and pluck the other end with your finger.

The ruler 1. ____________ and makes the air around it 2. ____________ too.

The 3. ____________ air carries the 4. ____________ to the ear.

The greater the vibration is, the louder the sound.

B. Try the experiments to see whether or not sound travels through different media. Circle the correct word and answer the questions.

Sound Travels Through...

Experiment 1: Air (Materials: two spoons)

Bang two spoons together.

Can you hear the sounds of the spoons clinking? ________

Conclusion: Sound **can / cannot** travel through air.

Experiment 2: Water (Materials: a balloon and water)

Fill the balloon with water. Listen while someone speaks with their lips against the balloon.

Can you hear the speaker? ________

Conclusion: ______________________________

Experiment 3: Solid

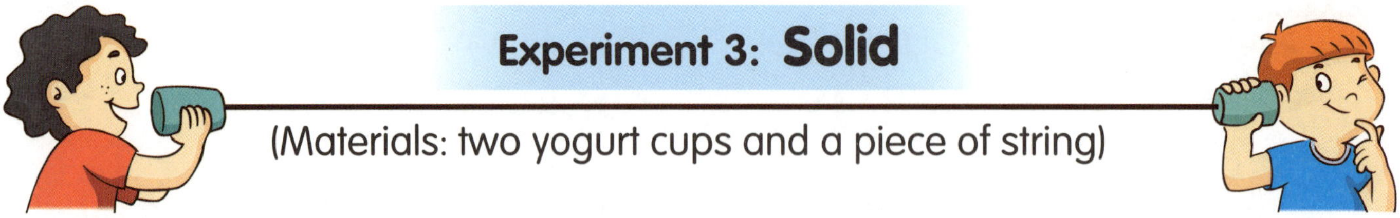

(Materials: two yogurt cups and a piece of string)

Poke a hole in the bottom of each cup. Thread the ends of a piece of string through the holes. Pull the string tight and tie a knot inside each cup.

Can your friend hear what you say when you speak into the cup? ________

Conclusion: ______________________________

C. Read the paragraph. Describe the sounds that the children make with the given words. Give examples of high- and low-pitched sounds.

If an object vibrates quickly, it makes a high-pitched sound. When you blow a whistle, the air inside vibrates quickly, making a high-pitched sound. However, if an object vibrates slowly, it makes a low-pitched sound. When a drummer hits the skin of a big drum, the skin vibrates slowly. This makes a low-pitched sound. Some things vibrate so fast or so slow that humans cannot even hear the sounds they make.

fast **slow**
high **low**

Sound from a Drum	**Sound from a Whistle**
1. Vibration: ______________	2. Vibration: ______________
Pitch: ______________	Pitch: ______________
Examples:	Examples:
• ______________	• ______________
• ______________	• ______________

5 What Happens to Sound

Sounds can be modified, reflected, or absorbed. In this unit, you will learn about how a sound's loudness is measured, and about how sound is reflected, absorbed, and modified. You will also learn about how a human ear works.

After completing this unit, you will

- know that the loudness of sound can be measured in decibels.
- understand how sound is modified, reflected, and absorbed.
- understand how the human ear works.

Vocabulary

modify: to change

reflect: to bounce back or off, like a sound wave bouncing off a wall as an echo

absorb: to take in, like a carpet dampening sounds in a living room

Extension

Have you ever noticed that the engine sounds of a rumbling truck become louder as the truck gets closer to you? Do you know why this happens?

Sound is caused by vibrations, and vibrations in air become weaker and weaker as they travel; therefore, sound is quieter far away than it is close up. The closer you are to a sound, the louder it is.

Look at an airplane in the sky. Can you hear any noise from the airplane? The airplane sounds quiet to you when it is up in the sky and you are on the ground.

A. Use the given words to fill in the blanks and complete the chart on the loudness of different sounds.

The 1. ____________ of a sound can be measured in 2. ____________ (dB).

decibels
loudness

a whisper
a jackhammer
a busy street

Sound	Loudness (dB)
airplane taking off	130
3.	110
someone shouting	100
a vacuum cleaner	80
4.	70
people talking	60
a quiet street	40
5.	30
a pin dropping	10

B. Fill in the blanks to show the properties of sound with the given words. Then circle the correct answers.

Properties of Sound

absorbed reflected modified pitch loudness

1. Sound can be r____________ from a **hard / soft** surface.
   - In a good concert hall, the right amount of reflected sound blending with direct sound makes the overall sound **poorer / richer** .
   - **An echo / Thunder** is an example of reflected sound.

2. Sound can be a____________ by a **hard / soft** surface.
   - **Carpeting / Wooden flooring** absorbs the sound of footsteps.
   - Music recording studios use sound **absorbing / reflecting** materials on their walls to eliminate any unwanted sound.

3. Sound can be m____________ .
   - L____________
     The harder you hit a drum, the **softer / louder** the sound it makes.
   - P____________
     The tighter the string of an instrument is, the **higher / lower** the pitch you get.

C. Fill in the blanks with the words from the diagram to complete the paragraph.

Sound waves are collected by the o__________ ear, which is made up of the __________, the __________, and the __________, a thin-skinned structure stretched tight like a drum that vibrates with sound waves. Waves travel through the ear canal and the eardrum to the m__________ ear. The middle ear's three __________ amplify the eardrum's vibrations and send them to the i__________ ear. Here, the snail-shaped __________ changes vibrations into signals that are carried by __________ to your brain.

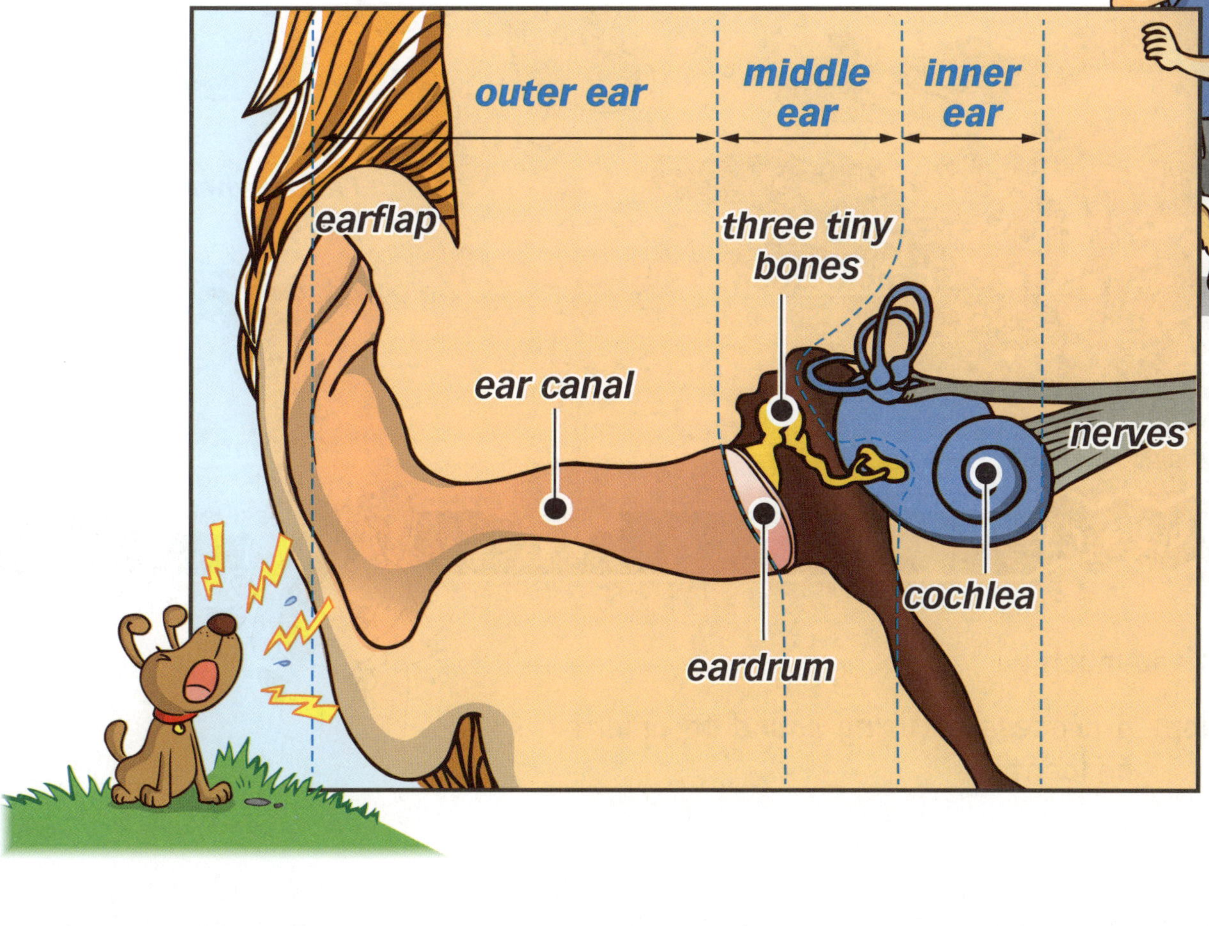

6 How We Use Light and Sound

We use light and sound all the time in everyday life. In this unit, you will see how we protect ourselves from excessive light and sound, how everyday items make use of the properties of light and sound, and how animals use sound.

After completing this unit, you will

- know some items that protect you from excessive light and sound.
- know some items that make use of the properties of light and sound.
- know what echolocation is.

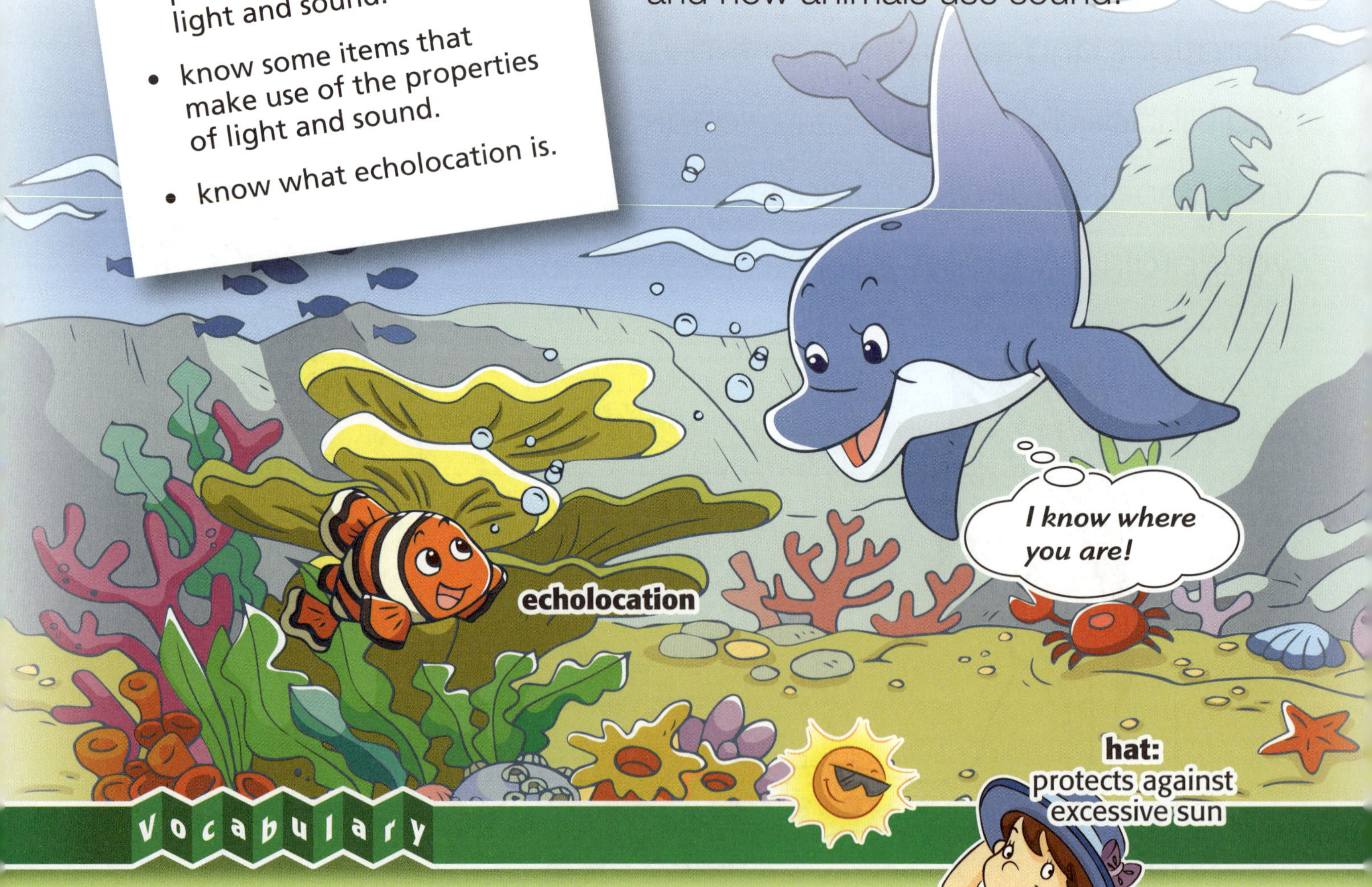

Vocabulary

excessive: too much

echolocation: a process of using sound to orient or locate

Extension

Sounds can tell us a lot about the world around us. They tell us when someone is calling us (a phone ringing), when it is lunch break at school (a bell ringing), and when it is time to wake up in the morning (an alarm clock ringing). Do you have some other ideas about how sound conveys messages?

Make a chart to list them out.

Source	Message Conveyed
ambulance	emergency (Get out of the way!)

A. Draw lines to show which items protect you from excessive light or sound. Then give a reason why it is important to protect yourself from excessive light or sound.

Protection from

Light •

Sound •

• sunscreen

• volume button

• patio umbrella

• earplug

____

____

B. Match the descriptions with the devices that make use of the properties of light or sound. Then fill in the blanks with "light" or "sound."

- **A** detects light and shadows; helpful at the grocery store
- **B** gathers and amplifies sound; helps people who have trouble hearing
- **C** turns sound waves into electrical energy; helps people talk to faraway friends and family
- **D** uses light energy to power its battery; helps people pay for parking
- **E** uses lenses to refract light in order to make objects appear closer; helps astronomers see the stars
- **F** turns sound waves into electrical energy; helps an audience hear someone on a stage

Devices That Use Light or Sound

1.

uses ____________

2.

uses ____________

3.

uses ____________

4.

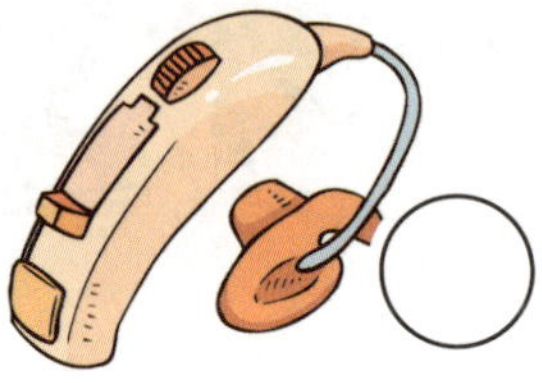

uses ____________

5.

: uses ____________

: uses ____________

C. Fill in the blanks with the given words to complete the paragraph.

surface	**echo**	**water**	**echolocation**
communicate	**air**	**sound**	**whale**

Like humans, animals use 1. ______________ to convey messages. Some bat and 2. ______________ species use something called 3. ______________ to find food, orient themselves, and 4. ______________ with one another. Echolocation involves an animal calling out and listening for an 5. ______________ – sound bouncing off a 6. ______________ – to know where the surface is. This way, animals can locate things like insects or fish. Bats send their calls through 7. ______________ , while whales send them through water. Both methods are effective, but whales have an advantage over bats: sound travels faster and farther in 8. ______________ than in air.

GRAY TOMATOES

understanding why tomatoes look red

Light is the reason we can see things around us. It usually looks white, but it is made up of different colors. However, the things that we can see are all different colors. What makes different objects under the same light appear as different colors? Why are things in certain colors? Why do we see tomatoes as red but not gray?

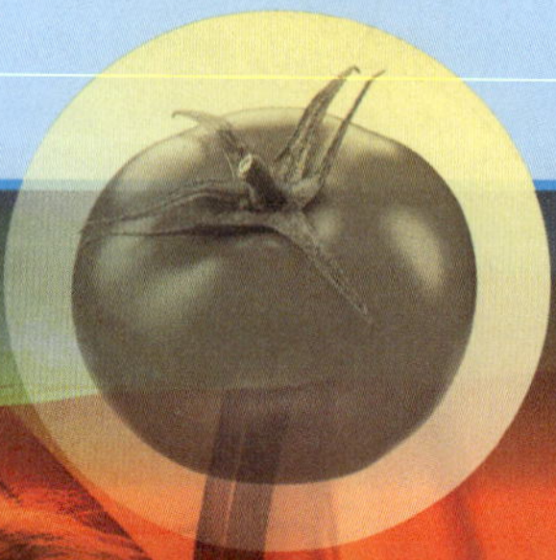

Difficulty:

●○○○○

Time needed:
10 minutes

In this experiment, you will explore why tomatoes look red.

What you need:

a flashlight

an elastic band

a red tomato

cellophane in green, yellow, and red

What to do:

1. Cover the flashlight with the green cellophane. Secure it with the elastic band.
2. Check the color of the tomato. Take the tomato with you into a dark room and put the tomato on a table.
3. Turn on the flashlight. Shine the flashlight on the tomato.
4. Check the color of the tomato. What color is it now?
5. Repeat this experiment with the yellow and red cellophane sheets.
6. Check the color of the tomato each time. What color did you see?

WHAT *just* happened?

The light from the flashlight passing through the cellophane appeared the same color as the cellophane. When you shone the green light on the tomato, the tomato looked gray; the same happened with the yellow light. But when the flashlight with the red cellophane was shone, the tomato looked red again.

Light Absorption

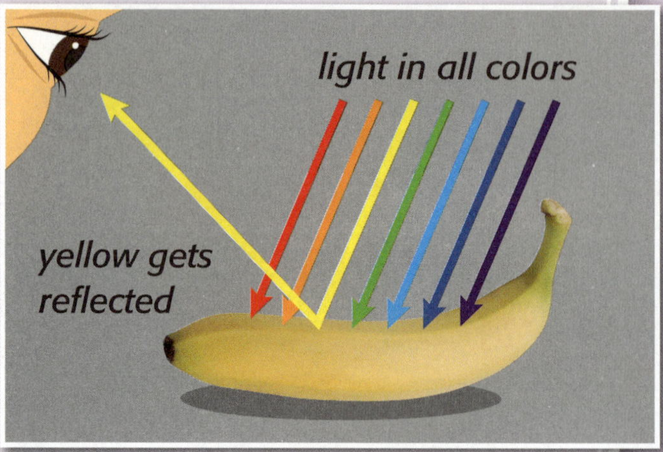

What made the tomato look gray? The tomato absorbed all lights except red light. When the green light hit the tomato, the tomato absorbed the green light and did not reflect it. Because no light was reflected, the tomato looked gray. The same thing happened with the yellow light. The tomato absorbed the yellow light and did not reflect it back, hence, the tomato appeared gray. However, when you used the red cellophane, you could see the tomato as red again. This is because when the red light hit the tomato, it reflected the red light instead of absorbing it.

Different objects have different colors because they reflect certain colors of light and absorb others. For a tomato, it absorbs green and yellow lights but reflects red light.

STEM INQUIRY

- Cover the flashlight first with the green cellophane sheet and then the red cellophane sheet on top. Shine it on a white surface. What color is the light? Switch the green and red cellophane sheets. What color is this light?

- Cover your camera lens or flash with a cellophane sheet. Shine it on different objects and observe what colors of the light are absorbed or reflected. Try this with cellophane sheets in different colors.
- Solar panels are a great invention. They absorb sunlight, a clean and renewable energy source, and convert it into electricity. Solar panels are usually in dark colors. Explain why.

- In the experiment, you used cellophane sheets as colored filters to test the light absorption properties. Can you make your own colored filters using other materials found around your home?

- Adjust the distance between the flashlight and the tomato, compare the level of light absorption and color change in the tomato. Make a chart like below to record your observations.

Distance (in/cm)	Color Change (most/medium/least)	Level of Light Absorption (high/medium/low)

LIGHT REFLECTION

understanding what happens when light hits mirrors

Have you ever wondered why you can see your reflection in a mirror? Light travels in a straight line and can bounce off an object like a ball bouncing off a wall. The object reflects the light into our eyes; therefore, we can see the object. Mirrors and other shiny surfaces are special because light hitting these surfaces at an angle reflects off at the exact same angle. This is why we can see our reflection clearly in a mirror.

Difficulty: ●○○○○

Time needed: 30 minutes

In this experiment, you will explore the concept of light reflection.

What you need:

a flashlight

an apple

aluminum foil

cardboard

What to do:

1. Cut two cards that are 8 in by 6 in (about 20 cm by 15 cm) out of the cardboard.
2. Wrap one card with a piece of smooth and flat foil with the shiny side facing out and the other card with a piece of crumpled foil.
3. Go into a dark room with the cards, the apple, and the flashlight.
4. Put the apple and the flashlight 40 in/1 m apart and 40 in/1 m away from a wall.

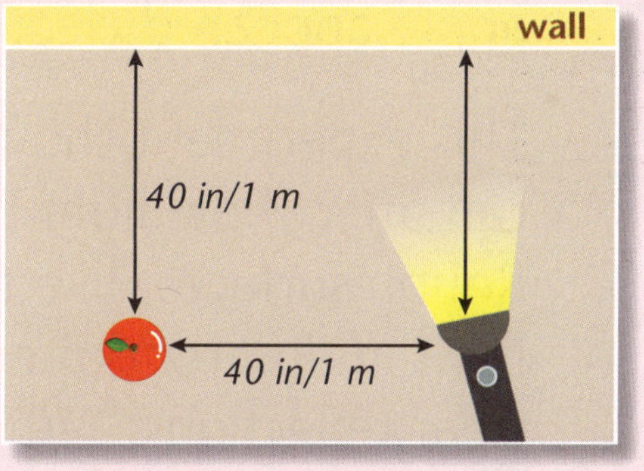

5. Place the card wrapped with the crumpled foil against the wall and shine the flashlight onto it.
6. Move and adjust the angle of the card to see whether you can see the apple itself being lit up and the reflection of the apple on the card.
7. Repeat Steps 5 and 6 using the card wrapped with the smooth and flat foil. Can you see the apple this time?

WHAT *just* happened?

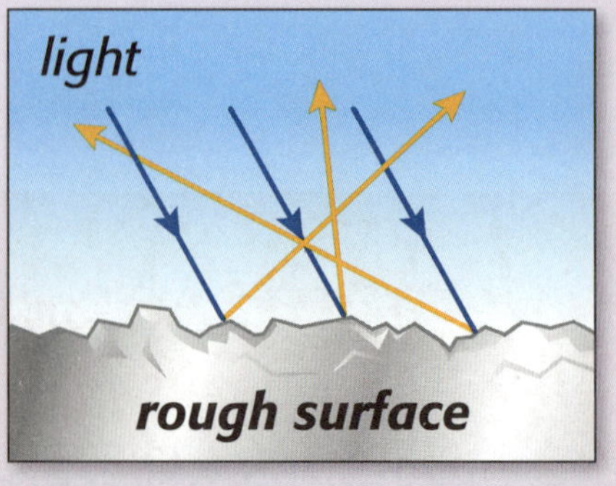

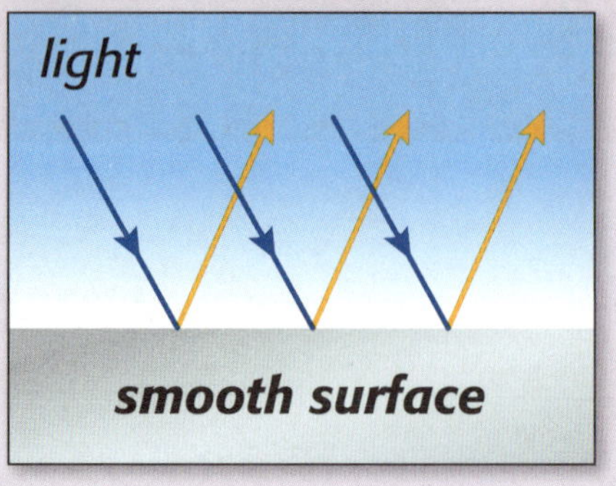

In this experiment, when the flashlight shone on the card wrapped with the crumpled foil, the rough surface caused the light to scatter in different directions. This made it difficult to see a clear reflection of the apple on the foil.

On the other hand, when the flashlight shone on the card wrapped with the smooth foil, the light hit the card and was reflected off at the same angle. The smooth and flat surface of the foil allowed the light to bounce off in the same direction. Therefore, the image of the apple appeared clearly on the card.

This experiment showed that the surface of an object can affect how light behaves when it hits the surface. Rough surfaces, like the crumpled foil, scatter the light in different directions, making it harder to see clear reflections. Whereas smooth surfaces, like the smooth foil, reflect the light more uniformly, allowing us to see clear reflections.

Knowing how light interacts with different surfaces helps us understand why some objects appear shiny, while others look dull or rough.

STEM INQUIRY

- What are some other materials that show good reflections of objects?

- Optical fibers are thin fibers that use light reflection to transmit light and information over a long distance. Do some research and find videos online with the permission from an adult to see how light bounces off the fiber's walls.

- If you are asked to build your own bedroom, will you use fairly smooth or textured surface for the floor and walls? Why?
- Design and build your own small-scale mirror maze. Adjust the angle of position of each mirror. Shine a flashlight on it. Observe the reflection and the light path.

- Look into a mirror. How is symmetry related to the reflected image in the mirror?

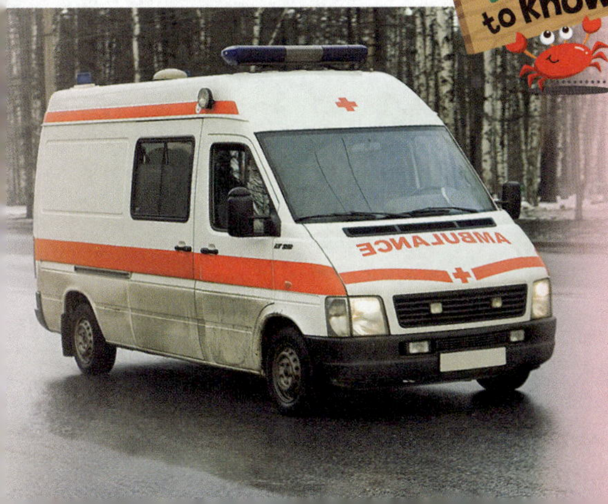

Fun to know

What Is "ƎƆИA⅃UꓭMA"?

Have you ever wondered why the word in the front of an ambulance is spelled backward? This is because it is meant to be read in the rearview mirror of cars in front of the ambulance. Since it is seen through a mirror, "ƎƆИA⅃UꓭMA" will be read as "AMBULANCE" for drivers.

BENDING LIGHT

understanding light refraction

Have you ever noticed that you move slower in water than in air? This happens to light too. When light enters water, it not only slows down but also bends at an angle. This bending is called refraction. Lenses use refraction to help us see things that we normally cannot see with our eyes alone. For example, lenses in binoculars help us see objects far away and lenses in microscopes help us see very small things.

What you need:

2 identical glass jars

water

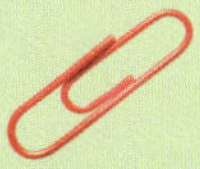

2 paper clips

2 pencils

Difficulty: ●○○○○

Time needed: 15 minutes

In these experiments, you will explore the refraction of light.

What to do:

Experiment 1

1. Place a pencil in each jar.
2. Fill one jar about three-quarters full with water.
3. Look at the pencil in each jar from the side. What did you see?

Experiment 2

1. Place a paper clip under each jar.
2. Fill one jar with water.
3. Look at the paper clip from the side of each jar at different angles. Did you notice that the paper clip under the jar with water could not be seen at certain angles?

STEM Note

100-square grid

$1 = 100\%$

$\frac{1}{100} = 1\%$

- $\frac{3}{4}$ of the grid filled
- 75 of 100 small squares filled

$$\frac{3}{4} = \frac{75}{100} = 75\%$$

WHAT *just* happened?

In the experiments, it might seem that optical illusion was at work. In fact, what the pencil and paper clip demonstrated was a phenomenon called light refraction – that is, when light travels from one medium to another, such as from air to water, it changes its speed and direction.

empty jar *jar filled with water*

In Experiment 1, the pencil in the empty jar looked straight. However, in the jar filled with water, the pencil appeared to be broken. In this case, when the pencil was in the water, the light from the pencil reached our eyes after passing through the water, the glass, and the air. As it crossed different media at different speeds, it changed directions. Because of this change in direction, our eyes perceived the pencil as being bent, making it appear to be broken.

empty jar *jar filled with water*

In Experiment 2, the paper clip under the jar filled with water seemed to disappear at certain angles also due to light refraction. Just like Experiment 1, as the light traveled through the glass, water, and air to reach our eyes, it got refracted. The light from the paper clip under the jar got bent in such a way that our eyes could not see the paper clip at certain angles.

STEM INQUIRY

- What is the difference between light reflection and light refraction?
- Refraction can sometimes put us at risk. When you look down to the bottom of a swimming pool from the edge and find it look shallow, does it mean it is safe to enter the water?

- Eyeglasses use light refraction to help people with vision problems see clearly. Do you know how they work? Research online with the permission from an adult to find out.

- In Experiment 2, you made the paper clip disappear to some extent. Can you design a decorative toy that shows different images when you look at it at different angles using the properties of light?

- In Experiment 1, hold the pencil in water such that it is perpendicular to the water surface and observe. Did the pencil look bent?

Fun to know

Electricity-free Light Bulbs

Have you ever heard of light bulbs that do not use electricity? In some countries where electricity is not readily available, people make light bulbs by using bottles filled with water and a bit of bleach (to prevent the growth of algae). When sunlight passes through the bottles of water attached to the roof, it gets refracted in all directions to light up dark rooms. This innovation helps people light up their rooms (with small or no windows) during the daytime without the use of electricity.

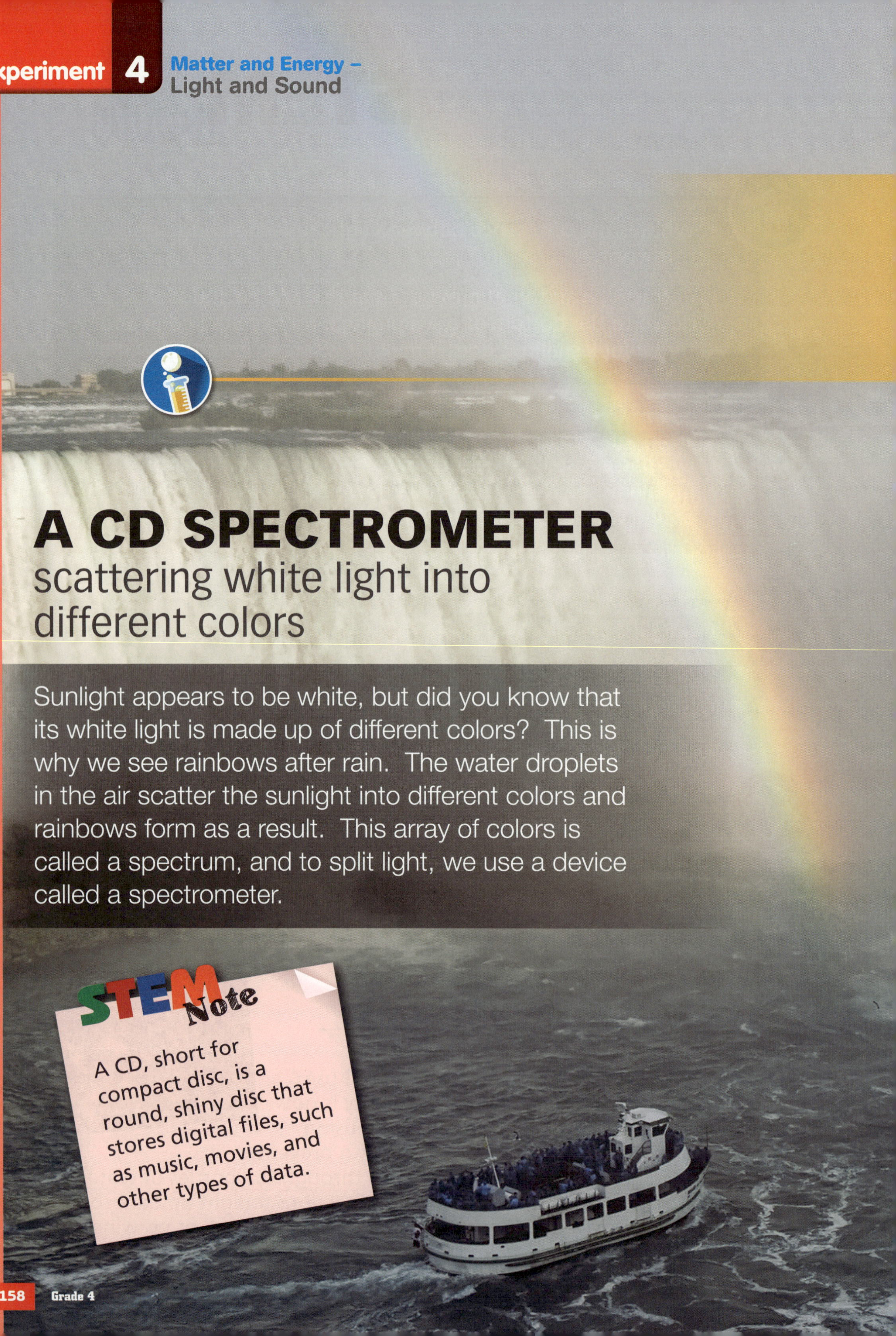

A CD SPECTROMETER

scattering white light into different colors

Sunlight appears to be white, but did you know that its white light is made up of different colors? This is why we see rainbows after rain. The water droplets in the air scatter the sunlight into different colors and rainbows form as a result. This array of colors is called a spectrum, and to split light, we use a device called a spectrometer.

STEM Note

A CD, short for compact disc, is a round, shiny disc that stores digital files, such as music, movies, and other types of data.

Difficulty: ●●●●○

Time needed: 1 hour

In this experiment, you will learn to make a CD spectrometer and use it to split light.

What you need:

a cardboard tube

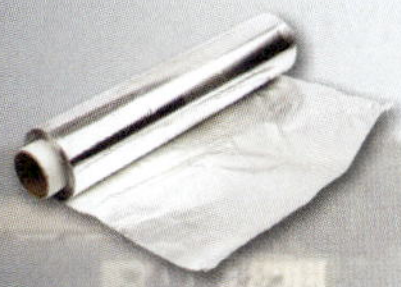
aluminum foil

a CD

scissors

What to do:

1. 

At one end of the cardboard tube, cut a slit about halfway through at a 45° angle.

2. 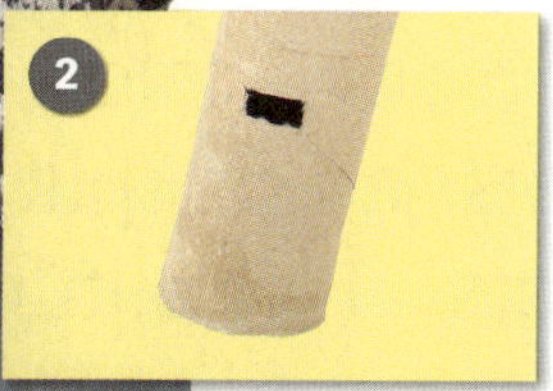
Cut a small eye hole directly opposite the slit.

3. 

Cover the top of the tube with a piece of aluminum foil. Cut a small slit in the center.

4. 
Insert the CD into the slit on the tube with the shiny side facing up. Then hold the tube under a light source and look through the eye hole. What did you see?

WHAT *just* happened?

CD Spectrometer

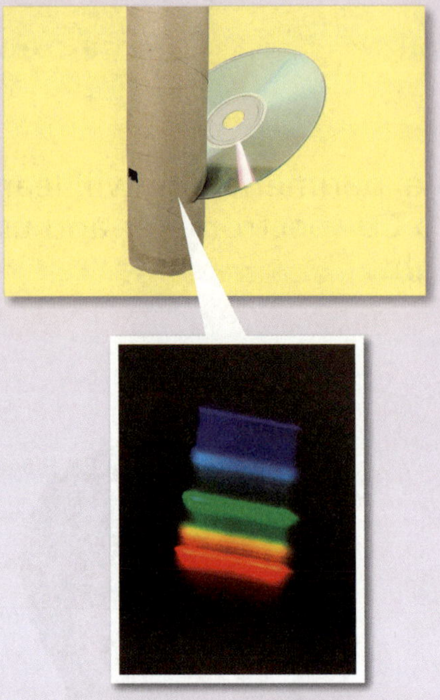

rainbow in the tube

When you looked through the eye hole of the tube, you should have seen a beautiful rainbow. The rainbow was formed because the CD has many tiny spiral pits on its surface. When light hit these pits, it scattered and spread out into different colors, creating a rainbow. This is similar to how water droplets scatter sunlight to form rainbows.

In the experiment, the CD spectrometer acted as a device that splits the white light, which is a combination of lights of all colors, into individual colors, such as red, yellow, and blue. The CD spectrometer is like a magical tool that reveals the hidden colors within light. In fact, different lights can be split into different combinations of colors. Try splitting different lights (e.g. sunlight, LED light, and incandescent light) with your CD spectrometer.

STEM INQUIRY

- Was the order of colors you observed the same in all rainbows? List the colors in order.
- What type of energy was used in this experiment?
- When light hits an object, it can be transmitted, reflected, or absorbed. Which of those was demonstrated in this experiment?
- What are some other objects that split white light into colors?

- How are colors combined to make new colors? Name the different ways.
- Come up with more ways to split light into individual colors, apart from using a CD spectrometer.

- Sketch a 45° angle. What benchmarks can you use to sketch the angle?
- What tools can you use to measure angles?

Fun to know

Why Is the Sky Blue?

Have you ever wondered why the sky is blue on a clear sunny day? This is because when the sun is high in the sky, blue light is scattered in all directions. The air molecules (extremely small particles) scatter more blue light than other colors; therefore, the sky is blue on a clear sunny day.

SOUND TRAVELS

understanding that sound can travel through different media

It is certain that hitting an object will produce sound. Once an object is hit, it vibrates and causes air around it to vibrate as well. These vibrations reach our ears and allow us to hear the sounds. Do you think sound can travel through other media besides air?

What you need:

scissors

string

a metal spoon

Difficulty: ●○○○○

Time needed: 5 minutes

In this experiment, you will learn that sound can travel through things.

What to do:

1. Tie the spoon in the middle of the string.
2. Hold the string and swing it slowly so that the spoon gently bangs against the edge of a table.
3. Hold the ends of the string close to your ears. Again, swing the spoon gently. Listen carefully.

STEM Note

Between a metal spoon and a plastic spoon, the metal spoon is used in this experiment so that the result will be obvious. In general, metal carries sound waves better than plastic does. When sound waves hit metal, the metal transmits vibration easily, producing a louder sound. On the other hand, plastic absorbs some of the sound, causing it to vibrate less and resulting in a quieter sound.

WHAT *just* happened?

As expected, when the spoon hit the table, you heard a clear sound from the string. To begin with, when the spoon was struck against the table, it vibrated. Vibrations are tiny movements traveling back and forth, just like when you wiggle your fingers really fast. The vibrations created by the spoon traveled from the spoon through the air and reached your ears. Your ears detected these vibrations and turned them into the sound you heard.

Interestingly, sound does not travel only through air, but also through other materials. When you placed the ends of the string against your ears, the vibrations from the spoon traveled through the string and reached your ears. The string acted as a pathway, carrying the vibrations from the spoon straight to your ears. Therefore, it allowed you to hear the sound too.

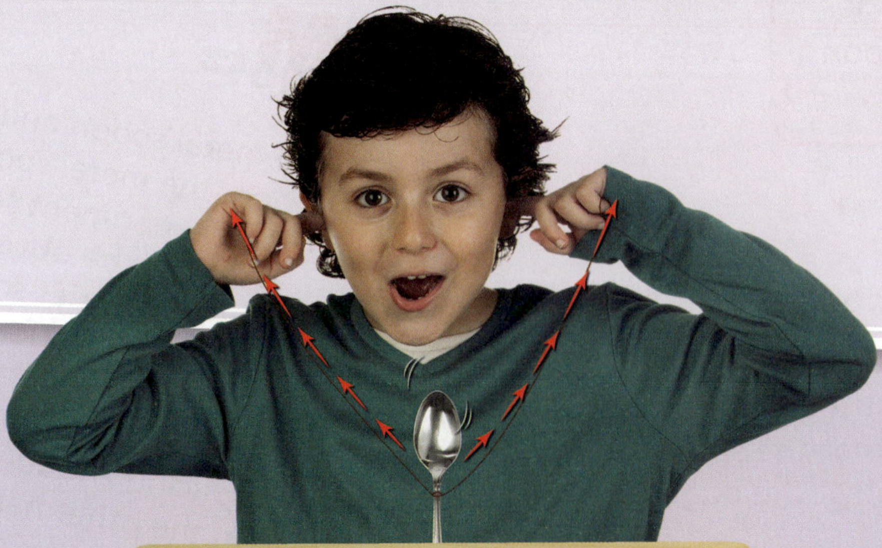

Vibrations from the spoon travel through the string and reach the ears.

STEM INQUIRY

- Instead of the metal spoon, what else can you use to conduct the experiment?
- Try hitting different objects or surfaces with the spoon. Compare the sounds you hear through the string.
- How does sound travel through air, solids, and liquids?

- How are sounds measured? Research online with the permission from an adult to find out about sound level meters and the noise regulations in your city.

- Can you make a simple string telephone? What can you do to improve the sound quality and its travel distance?

- Repeat the experiment by using strings at different lengths: 20 in (about 50 cm), 30 in (about 75 cm), and 40 in (about 100 cm). Compare the sounds you hear. Describe the differences, if any, of the sounds you hear through the strings.

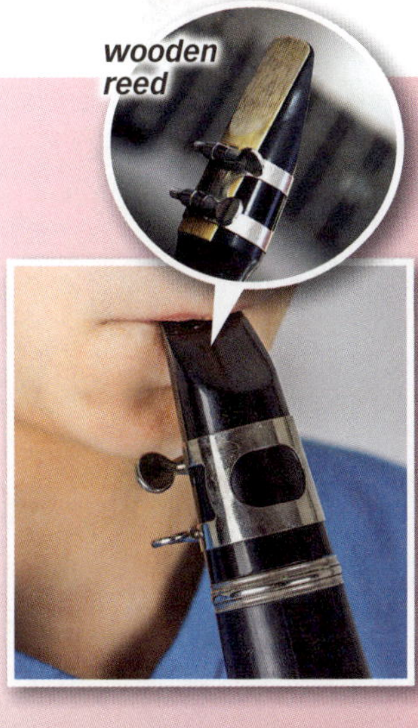

Fun to know

Music from Blowing

Instruments like drums, xylophones, and pianos make music when struck, but there are also instruments such as clarinets and trumpets that make music when blown. Typically, air that is blown into a clarinet strikes a piece of wood called reed, causing it to vibrate and make sound.

HEARING SOUNDS

comparing sounds that travel through different media

Ask your parent or a friend to help you out with this experiment.

Sound is all around us. No matter whether we are in a park or underwater, we can hear different types of sounds. Some sounds, like thunder, are loud, and some, like birds' chirping, are high-pitched. Sound can travel through the air, as well as other different media. But do sounds still sound the same when they go through different media?

Difficulty:
●●○○○

Time needed:
45 minutes

In this experiment, you will compare sounds traveling through different media.

What you need:

a large bowl

water

a plate

a plastic spoon

What to do:

1. Ask your helper to hold the plate and the spoon.
2. Cover one of your ears and compare the sounds that you hear in the following trials. Record your observations on the next page.

Trial 1:
Have your helper hit the plate gently with the spoon beside you.

Trial 2:
Have your helper hit the plate gently with the spoon while the plate is touching your uncovered ear.

Trial 3:
Fill the bowl with water. Submerge your ear slightly in the water. Have your helper hit the plate with the spoon beside you.

My Record

Loudness

Trial 1

soft loud

Trial 2

soft loud

Trial 3

soft loud

WHAT *just* happened?

The sound traveled through the air (gas) to reach your ear in Trial 1, through the plate (solid) in Trial 2, and through the water (liquid) in Trial 3. You should have heard the loudest sound in Trial 2.

As mentioned, sound must vibrate through a medium in order for it to spread. Solid media are denser, which makes it the easiest for vibrations to travel through them. This is why sounds are the loudest when heard through solid media. Liquid media, on the other hand, are less dense than solid media but denser than gaseous media. For this reason, the sound from Trial 3 was the second loudest.

STEM INQUIRY

- Why should your helper hit the plate gently with the plastic spoon?
- Sound waves are like invisible ripples that travel through different media. How are sound waves created?
- Some animals use sound primarily to navigate. Name some of these animals.

- Diagnostic ultrasound is an imaging method that uses sound waves. How is ultrasound used to help find and diagnose medical issues?

- A soundproof item is designed to prevent sounds from entering or leaving. Design a pair of soundproof headphones. Consider what properties you look for in the types of materials you choose.

Fun to know

Sonar – Using Sound to "See"

Sonar (**so**und **n**avigation **a**nd **r**anging) is used to help us explore and map the ocean with sound. Scientists use sonar by sending out sound waves into the water. Once the sound hits an object, it returns an "echo" to the sonar transducer, which can determine the range and orientation of the object. This is how we use sound to "see" the bottom of the ocean.

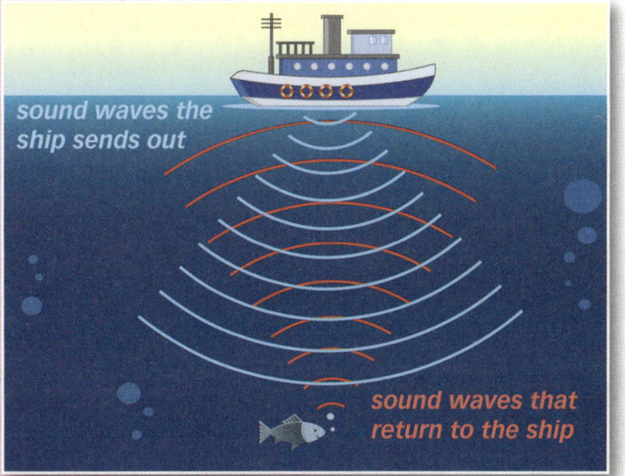

REFLECTORS AND ABSORBERS

understanding that sound can be reflected and absorbed

If you shout in a tunnel, you will hear your own loud voice as well as your echo. If you shout the same way but in a room that has curtains, couches, and carpeted floor, you will probably not hear an echo and your shout will sound softer. This happens because sound, like light, can be reflected and absorbed. But what things can reflect sound? What things can absorb sound?

What you need:

a cardboard tube

aluminum foil

an elastic band

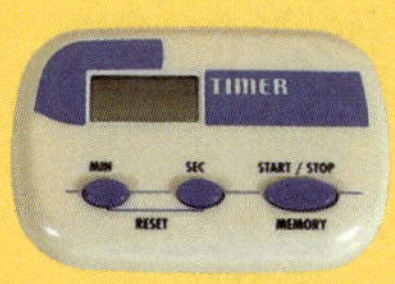

an alarm

Difficulty: ●●○○○

Time needed:
30 minutes

In this experiment, you will explore that sound can be reflected and absorbed.

What to do:

1. Cover one end of the tube with the aluminum foil and secure it with the elastic band.

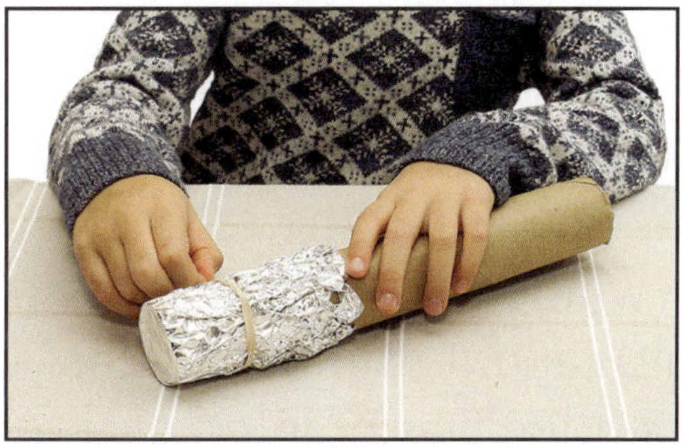

2. Turn on the alarm. Place it in the tube.

3. Point the open end of the tube at the surfaces of different materials listed in the chart on the next page.
4. Record your results.

STEM Note

Aluminum foil is made from aluminum, which is a lightweight and nonmagnetic metal.

My Record

Material	 Cabinet	 Window	 Curtain	 Carpet
Properties • hard • soft • smooth • porous				

When the tube was pointed at

- hard and smooth materials, the sound was **louder / softer** .
- soft and porous materials, the sound was **louder / softer** .

WHAT *just* happened?

You should have found that the alarm sounded louder when the tube was pointed at the cabinet and the window (hard and smooth materials), and it sounded softer when the tube was pointed at the curtain and the carpet (soft and porous materials). This is because hard and smooth materials are good at reflecting sounds, making sounds that reach the surfaces bounce back directly. Soft and porous materials, however, are good at absorbing sounds. The tiny holes inside them trap sounds, which muffle the sounds.

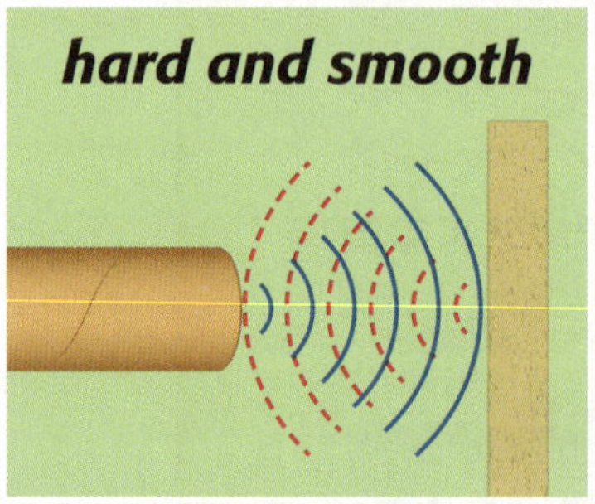

Almost all sound waves are reflected.

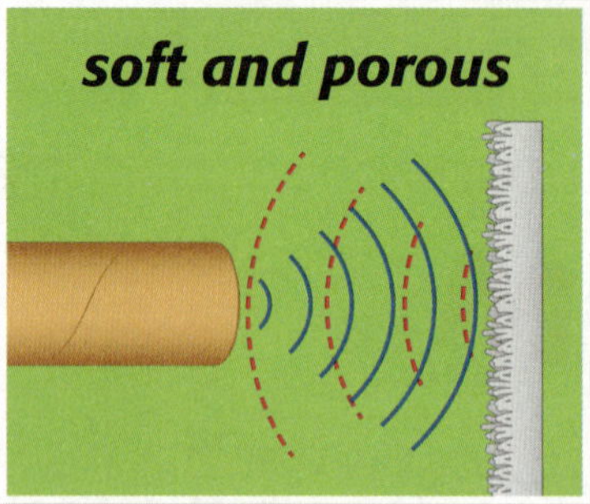

Some sound waves are absorbed and some are reflected.

STEM INQUIRY

- What are some other materials you can test in this experiment?
- How does sound travel to your ear?
- What is an echo? How does it occur?

- Sound amplifying is the process of making sounds louder. How does an amplifier amplify sound?

- Using materials from your home, design a tool that can amplify music played from a cell phone.

- Does the length of the tube in the experiment affect sound? If so, how?

Fun to know

Audible Pedestrian Signals

Do you know that sound is used at crosswalks to signal to pedestrians that it is safe to cross? The sounds from these signals change to indicate different stages of crossing, such as "start crossing" or "do not cross" signals. For people who are visually impaired, audible pedestrian signals are crucial to cross roads safely.

Section 4

Earth and Space Systems

1 Rocks and Minerals

Rocks build the land around us, and minerals make up the rocks. In this unit, you will see that rocks form much of our landscape. You will also learn about some of the characteristics of rocks and minerals, exploring the world of geology.

Vocabulary

diamond (a mineral)

mineral: a natural, solid, inorganic material with a specific chemical makeup and a crystal structure

rock: a natural, solid, inorganic material made of one or more minerals

geology: the study of Earth

inorganic: not living or never lived

Extension

Have you seen the stone landmarks built by the Inuit, the indigenous people of the Arctic region? These landmark structures, called inukshuks, have been used for navigation or as a point of reference for many years. They are either a single stone positioned in an upright manner or many rocks piled high in the shape of a human figure. Since rocks are strong materials, these structures can stay upright for years.

You can collect some rocks and balance them to build your own inukshuk. Then explore different ways in which you can make your structure stable.

A. Check all the places where you can find rocks. Then give one example of your own.

- (E) beach
- (F) garden soil
- (G) desert
- (H) cave
- (I) water
- (J) underground
- (K) volcano
- (L) forest floor
- ✔ ____________________

B. Complete the descriptions with the given words. Then answer the questions.

Type	Characteristic		Example
mineral	crystal	inorganic	
rock	natural	minerals	

diamond

sandstone

1. Type:

- solid, natural, ____________
- specific chemical makeup
- ____________ structure
- e.g. ____________

Type:

- solid, ____________ , inorganic
- made up of one or more ____________
- e.g. ____________

2. What makes rocks and minerals similar?

____

3. What makes them different?

____

4. Identify each as a rock or a mineral.

____________ ____________ ____________

C. Read the paragraph. Then fill out the geology fact card.

Geology is the study of Earth, including its origin, evolution, and fundamental structure. Many geologists study rocks and minerals, as rocks and minerals are some of the best clues to understanding what happened on Earth in the past, what is happening now, and what will happen. Rocks and minerals can tell geologists about everything from land movement billions of years ago, to what is at the center of Earth, to where earthquakes are likely to happen and when volcanoes are likely to erupt.

Geology Fact Card

Focus of Geology:	Things that rocks and minerals can tell geologists about:
1. ______________	• 3. ______________
______________	• 4. ______________
______________	• 5. ______________
Things that many geologists study:	• 6. ______________
2. ______________	
______________	

2 Minerals

Geologists find ways to classify thousands of minerals on Earth. In this unit, you will learn about how to classify minerals by their properties and test the properties of minerals.

After completing this unit, you will

- know the properties that are used to identify minerals.
- know some tests used to identify the physical properties of minerals.

Vocabulary

luster: the way that light reflects off the surface of a mineral

transparency: how well light can pass through a mineral

hardness: how difficult it is to scratch a mineral

streak: the color of a mineral's powder

Extension

Minerals are not just buried deep in rocks; they can be found around your home! In the kitchen, you might find table salt (mineral: halite), aluminum foil (mineral: aluminum), and copper pots (mineral: copper). In your pencil case, you might find pencil cores made of a mineral called graphite. Check to see what minerals you might find in your home.

A. Write the properties that we can use to identify minerals and describe them with the given words.

luster
color
streak
hardness
transparency
dull soft
translucent

Properties of Minerals

1. ______________ : how well light can pass through a mineral; e.g. opaque, ______________ , and transparent

2. ______________ : the way that light reflects off a mineral's surface; e.g. metallic, glassy, waxy, and ______________

3. ______________ : a mineral's color; e.g. red, green, and purple

4. ______________ : how difficult it is to scratch a mineral; e.g. hard and ______________

5. ______________ : the color of a mineral's powder; e.g. white, brown, and black

B. What properties of minerals do the tests reveal? Write the answers on the lines. Then write to match the mineral samples with their descriptions and circle the correct words.

Test 1 Scratching a mineral with another mineral

Property Revealed: 1. ____________________

Test 2 Rubbing a mineral on a rough surface to see the color of the powder left

Property Revealed: 2. ____________________

Test 3 Observing how light interacts with a mineral

Properties Revealed: 3. ____________________

Mineral Samples

4. ____________ mineral
- green
- leaves a bluish streak
- **metallic / waxy**
- **opaque / transparent**

5. ____________ mineral
- yellow
- leaves a yellow streak
- **metallic / glassy**
- **translucent / opaque**

6. ____________ mineral
- colorless
- leaves a white streak
- **glassy / dull**
- **translucent / opaque**

C. Read the paragraph. Then complete the Mohs hardness scale and answer the questions.

The Mohs hardness scale lists certain minerals from 1 to 10, with 1 being the softest and 10 being the hardest. A mineral has the ability to scratch another mineral that is softer but not one that is harder. Every mineral is given a hardness number based on its ability to scratch and be scratched.

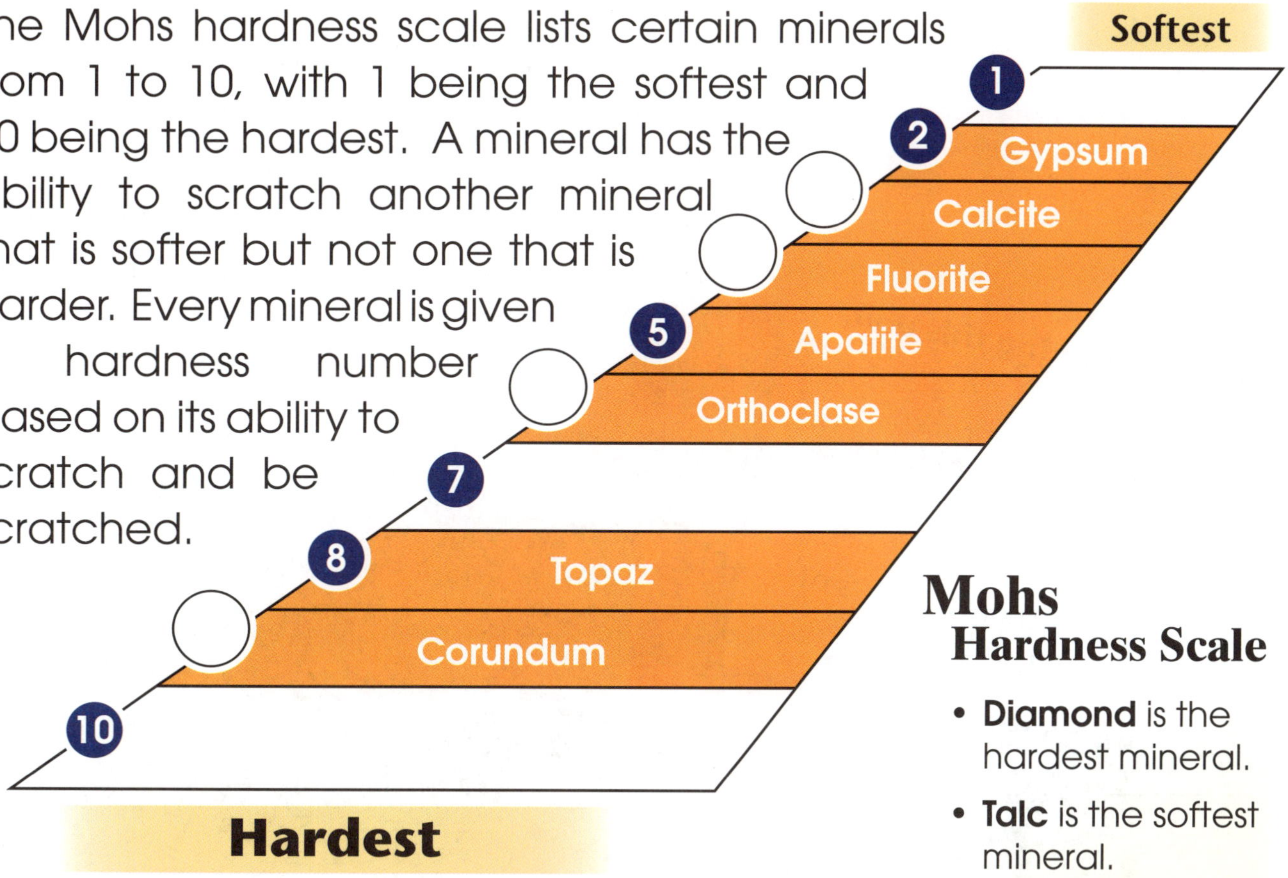

Mohs Hardness Scale

- **Diamond** is the hardest mineral.
- **Talc** is the softest mineral.
- **Quartz** is harder than orthoclase but softer than topaz.

1. Corundum can be scratched by ______________ .

2. Your fingernail has a hardness of 2.5 and can scratch ______________ and ______________ .

Never test good mineral samples or anything of high value, such as jewelry, because the damage caused by a scratch could be permanent.

3. Name two minerals that can be scratched by a mineral with a hardness of 6.5.

____

3 Rocks

There are many different types of rocks around you. They are made of different materials and were formed in different ways. In this unit, you will learn about the three main types of rocks: igneous, sedimentary, and metamorphic.

After completing this unit, you will

- understand that rocks have unique characteristics that are a result of how they were formed.
- know the characteristics of the three types of rocks.

Vocabulary

magma: liquid rock underground

lava: liquid rock aboveground

fossil: a trace of a living thing preserved in rock

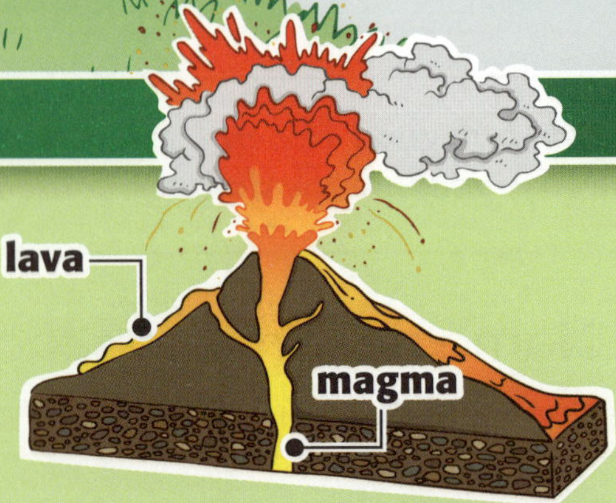

Extension

You can walk around your community and collect different rock samples. An egg carton is a great place to store your rocks, but first, use an old toothbrush and some water to clean each rock sample. Then observe the colors and luster of the rocks, make streaks, and feel their textures. Number the rocks and record their information.

A. Draw lines to match each rock type with its compositions.

Types of Rocks

Compositions

- igneous or sedimentary rocks
- sediment – pebbles, sand, mud
- magma (liquid rock beneath Earth's surface) or lava (liquid rock that comes to Earth's surface)

B. Identify the different types of rocks. Fill in the blanks with the given words and write the examples.

Types of Rocks

metamorphic igneous sedimentary

Examples

obsidian
volcanic black glass

gneiss
was once granite

marble
was once limestone

granite
visible crystals and very grainy

sandstone
layers of sand pressed together

Types of Rocks

1. [______________ rock]

lava	**magma**
small	**cools**

a. **intrusive**

- formed when ______________ cools and hardens below Earth's surface
- magma ______________ slowly, so rocks have a shiny, grainy texture and form large mineral crystals
- e.g. ______________

b. **extrusive**

- formed when ______________ cools and hardens on Earth's surface
- lava cools quickly, so rocks have ______________ crystals or no crystals
- e.g. ______________

2. [________ rock]

under fossils layers

- formed when pressure from ________ of sediment presses the layers below and dissolved minerals in water bind layers together

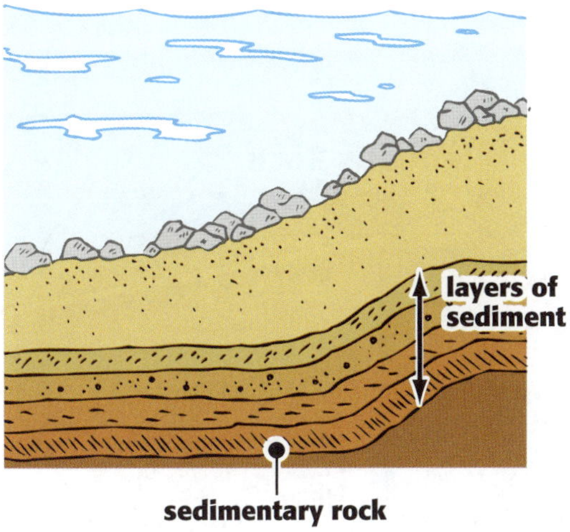

- often formed ________ water
- most rocks have layers and some have ________
- e.g. ________

3. [________ rock]

rarely extreme

- formed when rock is transformed into another type of rock by ________ temperatures and pressure below Earth's surface
- these rocks ________ have fossils because the heat needed to transform rock would destroy them
- e.g. granite (igneous rock) limestone (sedimentary rock)

____

____

4 The Rock Cycle

Together, igneous, sedimentary, and metamorphic rocks form a cycle. In this unit, you will learn about the rock cycle. You will see how processes like melting, applying extreme heat and pressure, and erosion act on rocks to transform them.

After completing this unit, you will

- know what erosion is.
- understand how the rock cycle happens.
- know some examples of rock transformations.

Vocabulary

erosion: the breaking off, breaking down, and moving of rock due to natural forces or human activities

extreme: intense

pressure: the force that presses on an object

Extension

When you visit a beach, pick up some pebbles and check their size, shape, and texture. Take a close-up picture of each of them. Then compare them with pebbles you find in your backyard or around your neighborhood.

You may find that the edges of the beach pebbles are rounder and smoother than the pebbles in your neighborhood. Do you know what causes the beach pebbles to become round and smooth?

A. Fill in the blanks with the given words.

erosion	sand	mountains	sedimentary
	cycle	moving water	

Erosion

Pebbles, 1. ________________ , clay, and silt come from larger rocks, which can come from landforms like 2. ________________ . Glaciers, landslides, 3. ________________ , and plant roots break off or break down rocks, causing 4. ________________ . All three types of rocks can be eroded into small pieces and eventually settle into the sea to become 5. ________________ rocks. Erosion destroys rocks and is an important part of the rock 6. ________________ .

B. Look at the rock cycle diagram. Fill in the blanks and answer the questions.

The Rock Cycle

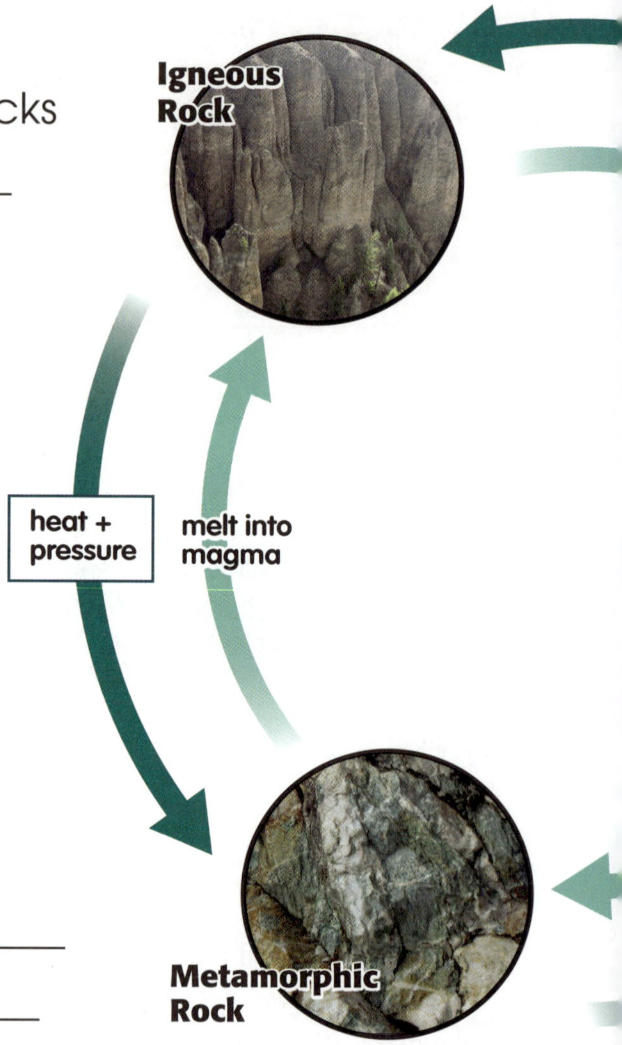

1. Igneous and ______________ rocks can become ______________ rocks under intense heat and pressure.

2. When ______________ and metamorphic rocks break down into small pieces and are carried away in a process called ______________, they can become ______________ rocks.

3. Metamorphic and ______________ rocks can become ______________ rocks if they melt into magma.

4. How do metamorphic rocks become igneous rocks?

____

5. How do sedimentary rocks become metamorphic rocks?

____

6. How do igneous rocks become sedimentary rocks?

____

7. What happens to sedimentary rocks when they are exposed to heat and pressure?

____

C. Read the paragraph. Then complete the diagram.

The rock cycle shows us that heat and pressure can turn both sedimentary and igneous rocks into metamorphic rocks. Here are some examples. Sandstone and limestone, common sedimentary rocks, turn into quartzite and marble respectively. Shale, a sedimentary rock made of silt, becomes slate. Granite, a common igneous rock, becomes gneiss.

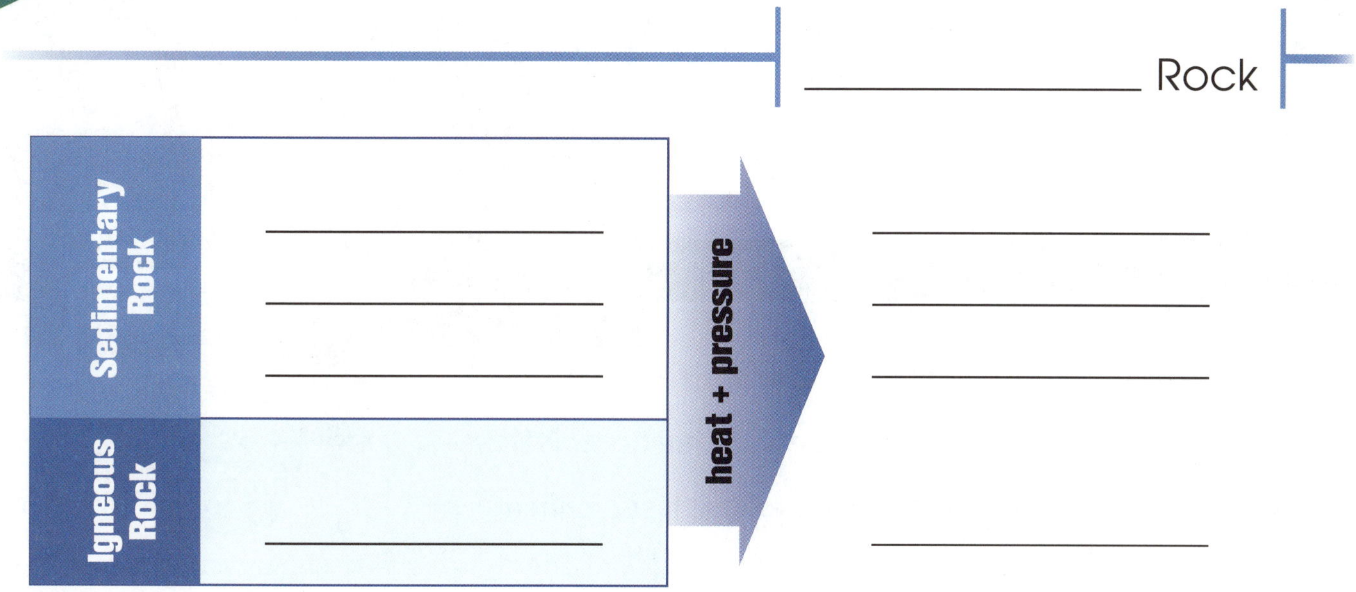

5 How We Use Rocks

Rocks are used in almost every aspect of life: building, art, electricity, and more. They are also important to paleontology, the study of prehistoric life. In this unit, you will learn about some of the many ways people use rocks.

After completing this unit, you will

- know where metals are found.
- understand why rocks are important to people.
- know what fossils are and understand why they are important to paleontologists.

Vocabulary

paleontology: the study of prehistoric life

metal: a type of minerals with special characteristics

ammonite: a fossilized shell of an extinct sea animal

Extension

Have you noticed that many things around you are made from rocks? The concrete foundation of your home, the glass of your windows, the tiles in your bathroom, and even the metal pipes moving heat and water through your home are made from rocks. Metals are found in rocks, and they are one of the most important materials we get from Earth. Check and list things in your home that are made from rocks or metals.

A. Fill in the blanks with the given words. Then circle the metals.

Metals

ore   quarries   minerals

Metals are found within 1. ____________ in rocks. When they are extracted from rock, the rock is called 2. ____________ . Metals, other minerals, and rocks are extracted from sites called mines or 3. ____________ .

a copper key

Metals

lead	salt	silver	nickel
gold	shale	sand	tin
iron	water	aluminum	oxygen

B. Write the correct heading to show the area of life in which rock is used. Then complete the descriptions with the given words.

jewelry energy art construction transportation

trains concrete coal diamonds colors oil steel sculptures

1. ______________

- Marble is a rock used for ______________ .
- The pigments that give paint ______________ come from minerals.

2. ______________

- Cars, airplanes, ships, and ______________ are made of ______________ and aluminum, which are metals.

3. ______________

- Steel from iron and ______________ from various rocks are important building materials.

4. ______________

- ______________ , a rock made from organic matter, is used for electricity and heat.
- ______________ can be extracted from the rocks beneath the ocean floor by an oil rig.

5. ______________

- Gold, silver, and ______________ make beautiful things.

C. Read the paragraph. Answer the questions. Then put the pictures in order from 1 to 4.

Paleontology is the study of prehistoric life. Paleontologists are able to study prehistoric life because of rocks. Rocks hold fossils, which are traces of things that lived long ago. Only sedimentary rocks provide the ideal conditions for fossils, as sediment slowly covers once-living organisms, mineralizes them, and turns into rock around them. Most fossils are never found, but erosion and human activities expose some, allowing paleontologists to do their work.

1. Why are rocks important to paleontologists?

____

____

2. What types of rocks hold fossils?

____

3.

Ammonite Fossil Formation

6 More about How We Use Rocks

The use of rocks is important to people, but the outcomes of this use can be both positive and negative. In this unit, you will see that the use of rocks affects people and the environment.

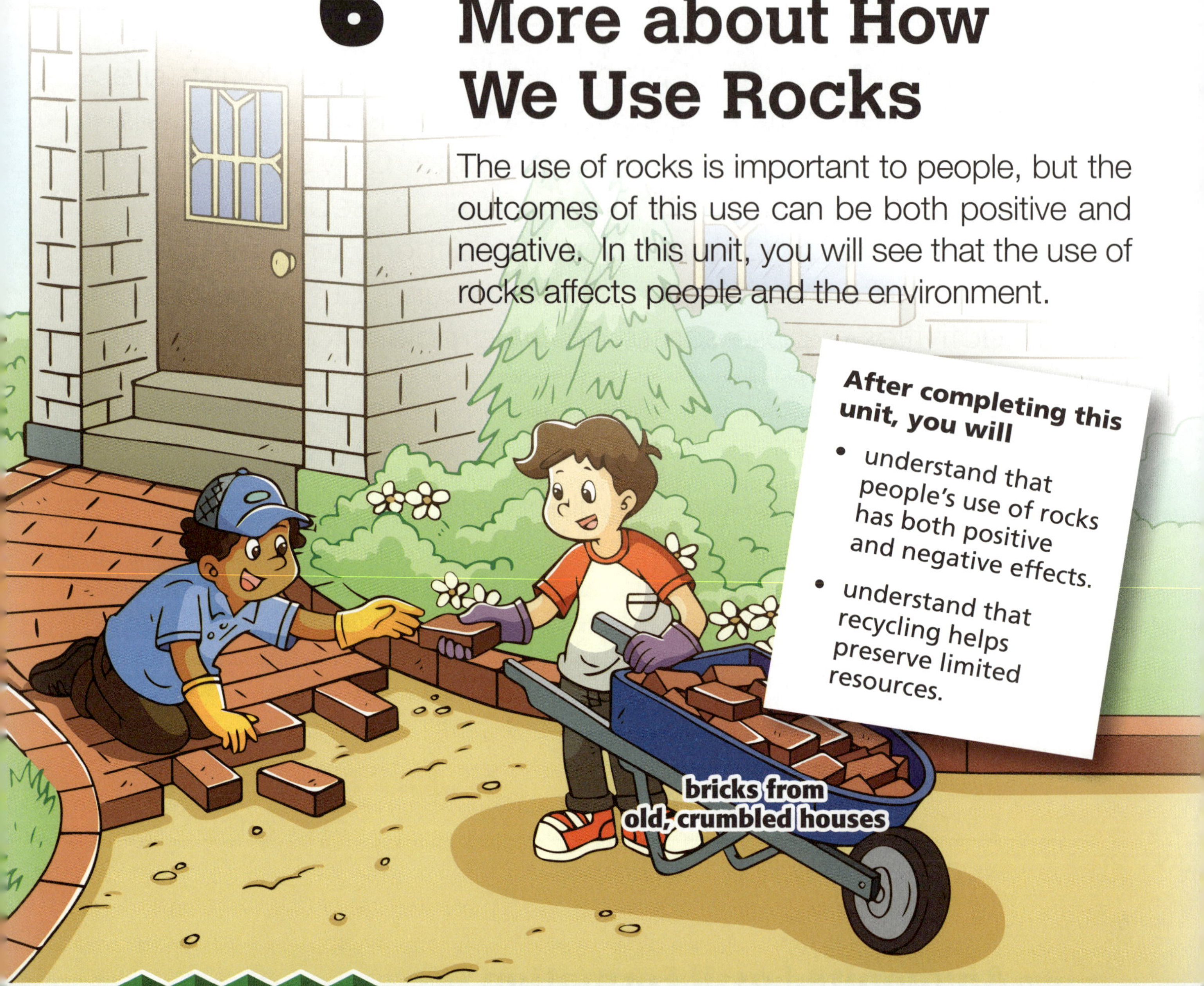

After completing this unit, you will

- understand that people's use of rocks has both positive and negative effects.
- understand that recycling helps preserve limited resources.

Vocabulary

recycle: to treat or process something to make it suitable for reuse

resource: something that can be drawn upon

raw material: a material found in nature

manufacture: to make a product from raw materials

Extension

Rocks are not just important parts of everyday products; they provide jobs for many people. Some people sell bricks, concrete, patio stones, and much more. Masons build houses with rock. Miners extract minerals and rocks from Earth. Factory workers make steel for cars and car parts, cans for food and drinks, and much more from rock. Interview your parents or neighbors to see if they work with rocks in some way.

A. Check the correct circles.

Impact That Quarries and Mines Have on Communities and Ecosystems:

Positive

- (A) create jobs
- (B) create habitats
- (C) cause damage to cars
- (D) quarried stone is used to make concrete for buildings
- (E) supply factories with raw materials
- (F) can be used as swimming pools

Negative

- (A) cause air and water pollution
- (B) destroy habitats
- (C) attract mice and other rodents
- (D) remove rich topsoil from the earth
- (E) disturb wildlife
- (F) support invasive species

B. Read the scenario. Decide whether each person is affected positively or negatively and explain your idea. Then write an example of one more person in the community who is affected and write how.

A mine has opened outside the Town of Big Rock, which is a place rich in metal and mineral resources. It provides people with jobs and the factory with raw materials to manufacture steel for cars. However, the mine disturbs the local habitat, and the residents of the Big Rock close by worry about how it will affect their drinking water.

1. **Factory Owner**: **positively / negatively** affected

   ____

   ____

2. **Resident of the Big Rock**: **positively / negatively** affected

   ____

   ____

3. **Miner**: **positively / negatively** affected

   ____

   ____

4. ____________ : **positively / negatively** affected

   ____

   ____

C. Fill in the blanks with the given words to complete the paragraph. Then answer the questions.

recycled | sixty | melted
aluminum | preserve | mining

Do you drink soda or juice from cans, and put your empty cans in a recycling bin? You should, because the 1. ____________ that cans are made from is one of the most recyclable materials on Earth. An empty can is 2. ____________ down, remolded, refilled, and back on grocery store shelves in as short as 3. ____________ days. Also, aluminum can be 4. ____________ again and again. Recycling aluminum is less expensive than 5. ____________ it, and not having to mine new aluminum helps us 6. ____________ our resources.

7. In what ways is recycling aluminum better than mining it?

____

____

8. Apart from aluminum, what made from rocks or minerals can be put in the recycling bin?

____

VOLCANOES
a violent explosion

Volcanoes are classified as active, dormant, or extinct depending on several factors including the history of volcanic activities and the potential to erupt in the future. Volcanic eruptions can have devastating effects on people and the environment, but they can also have positive impacts on an area, such as bringing rich, fertile soil and creating new islands.

STEM Note

The openings at the surface of volcanoes are called vents.

What you need:

baking soda

vinegar

a plastic bottle

modeling clay

a container

red food coloring

Difficulty:
●●●○○

Time needed:
2 hours

In this experiment, you will learn about why volcanoes erupt.

What to do:

1. Mold modeling clay around the plastic bottle in the shape of a volcano. Leave the mouth of the plastic bottle open. You can paint it brown and add some trees for a more realistic look.
2. Add two tablespoons of baking soda in the bottle.
3. Pour some vinegar into the container.
4. Add a few drops of the food coloring to the vinegar and mix them.
5. Pour the mixture into the vent of your volcano carefully.
6. Watch as your volcano erupts.

WHAT *just* happened?

Mixing the baking soda and vinegar in the bottle created an exciting reaction! When these two substances combined, they formed carbonic acid, which quickly broke apart into water and carbon dioxide. As the carbon dioxide gas was released, pressure built up inside the bottle. This pressure needed an escape – and this demonstrated why a volcano erupts.

However, volcanic eruptions are not caused by a chemical reaction as simple as what you saw in the experiment. In nature, due to the extreme heat deep underground, rock melts and becomes liquid rock. This liquid rock is called magma. Meanwhile, pressure keeps building up in the underground. When the pressure becomes strong enough, the magma searches for weak spots on Earth's surface to escape. When it finds a weak spot, it shoots out with incredible force – similar to what you saw in the experiment but in a much larger scale.

As magma rises up and makes its way to the vent, what finally comes out from a volcano is an extremely hot substance – lava. Lava glows with a bright, fiery red color and it is so hot that it can melt almost anything in its path.

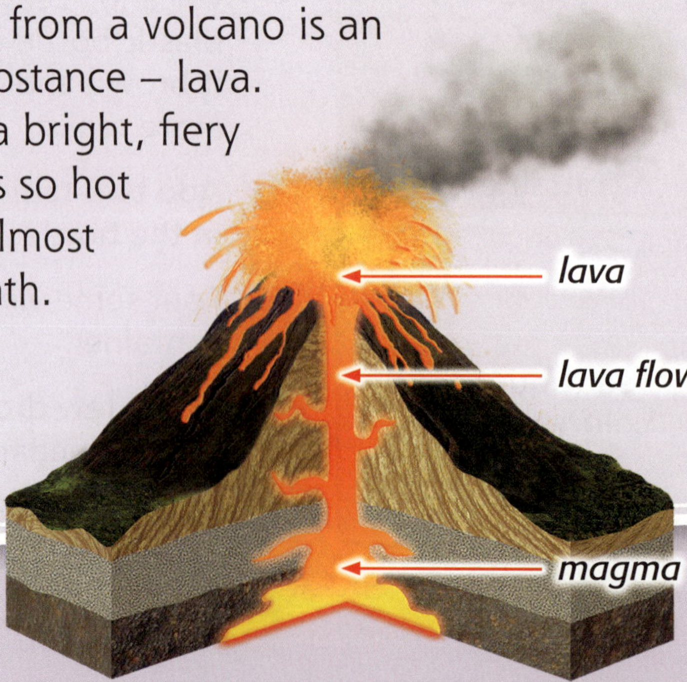

STEM INQUIRY

- What types of rocks are created by volcanic eruptions?
- How does the land around a volcano change as the volcano erupts?

- Research online with the permission from an adult in which continent are most volcanoes found.
- Volcanoes are classified as active, dormant, or extinct. An active volcano is one that has erupted recently or is expected to erupt in the near future. There are currently over 1,000 active volcanoes in the world. Many more volcanoes are dormant, meaning that they have not erupted in a long time but may erupt in the future, or extinct, which are not expected to erupt. Go online with the permission from an adult to find the volcano that is closest to your home. Find information about the volcano such as what type of volcano it is, how tall it is, and when it last erupted.

- Magma is extremely hot, commonly at 1,200˚F to 2,400˚F. Find the temperature range in degree Celsius.
- How far is the closest volcano to where you live? How long does it take you to travel to the volcano?

Fun to know

Fire-born Rocks

Igneous rock is formed when lava cools and hardens on or below Earth's surface after a volcanic eruption. Granite, an example of igneous rock, has a shiny and grainy texture with large mineral crystals. It is commonly used as a decorative building material for its beauty and durability.

GROWING MINERALS

understanding how minerals are formed in nature

Minerals are naturally-occurring materials. They are formed under intense heat and pressure, as well as from evaporation of liquids. Diamond, gold, and even salt are all examples of minerals.

What you need:

 sugar

 water

 a pot

 a wooden skewer

 a spoon

 food coloring

 a jar

 a binder clip

Difficulty:
●●●●○

Time needed:
1 week

In this experiment, you will learn about how minerals are formed.

CAUTION!
Ask an adult for help when handling hot water.

What to do:

1. Boil two cups of water in the pot on a stove.
2. Turn the heat off. Add sugar to the hot water.
3. Keep stirring and adding sugar until there is a small amount at the bottom of the pot that does not dissolve.
4. Fill two-thirds of the jar with the sugar water. Add a few drops of the food coloring into it.
5. Dip the pointed end of the wooden skewer in the water and roll it over some sugar. Let the skewer dry.
6. Put the wooden skewer back in the jar. Attach the other end of the skewer to the binder clip to keep it in place.
7. Leave the jar untouched. Observe the jar every day for a week. Can you see crystals growing?

WHAT *just* happened?

In this experiment, you witnessed the growth of sugar crystals on the skewer. It was possible because the sugar water was saturated, meaning it could not dissolve any more sugar.

As the saturated solution cooled down, it became more difficult for the water to hold onto the previously dissolved sugar. At the same time, the water in the bottle slowly evaporated, resulting in less water and leaving more sugar undissolved. So, little by little, the sugar separated from the water and started sticking together. As time went on, more and more sugar gathered around the skewer, arranging themselves in a specific way that created the crystals.

From this experiment, you have gained a glimpse of how minerals form naturally. In nature, the formation of minerals takes a long time – sometimes even thousands of years. The process can involve a combination of deposition of mineral-rich liquids, heat, and pressure.

- Why was it important to use hot water in the first place?
- Why was it important to roll the skewer over some sugar?
- Why do you think the sugar crystals only grew on the skewer but not throughout the entire jar?

- Take a photo of the crystals every 12 hour. Put the photos in order and compare.
- Name the minerals you know. Where can you find them? With the permission from an adult, research online with the permission from an adult to find out.

- Will you get similar results if you change the wooden skewer to a stainless steel skewer, string, or pipe cleaner? What properties of the skewer help the crystals grow?
- How do you speed up the formation of the crystals?
- What other crystals can you grow at home?

- Solubility is the ability of a substance to dissolve in another substance. Test the solubilities of different substances in water. Make a chart like the one below to record you results.

Solubilities of Different Substances

	Substance (oz/g)		
	Sugar	Salt	________
Amount Dissolved in $\frac{1}{2}$ Cup of Water			

SALT DAMAGE
effects of salt on plants

Did you know that salt is a mineral? Apart from making our food delicious, salt is also used to deice roads during the winter to improve road safety. Unfortunately, salt spray from passing cars and dissolved salt in runoff can damage plants.

What you need:

3 yogurt cups

soil

red beans

salt

water

a teaspoon

Difficulty:
●●●○○

Time needed:
2 weeks

In this experiment, you will explore how salt affects plants.

What to do:

1. Label the cups: "No Salt," "$\frac{1}{4}$ tsp Salt," and "$\frac{1}{2}$ tsp Salt."
2. Fill the cups with soil and plant a red bean in each.
3. Water the beans with tap water.
4. Once all the beans germinate, water the plants every day with the labeled amount of salt dissolved in two teaspoons of water.
5. Observe the plants. Measure and record the heights of the plants every day in the chart on the next page.

My Record

Heights of Plants

Day	1	2	3	4	5	6	7	8	9	10
No Salt										
$\frac{1}{4}$ tsp Salt										
$\frac{1}{2}$ tsp Salt										

WHAT *just* happened?

This experiment showed that the more salt was added to a plant, the poorer the plant grew. The salt dissolved in the water dominated other nutrients in the soil such as potassium and phosphorus; therefore, the plants did not have a balance of nutrients to support their growth. The plant labeled "½ tsp Salt" should have been the shortest in height. Apart from the height, the brownish leaves on the plant were another sign of salt damage to your plant.

The plant labeled "No Salt" was a controlled sample. It showed that plants without the presence of salt grew steadily. Now that you have learned the negative effects of salt on plants, what are you going to do to prevent plants from salt damage?

STEM INQUIRY

- What is the difference between road salt and table salt?
- How do you prevent plants from salt damage?
- Do you think ocean plants are salt tolerant?

- With the permission from an adult, research online with the permission from an adult to find out what plants are tolerant in salty soil and find some photos. With an adult, explore your neighborhood to see if anyone has planted them in their garden.

- How many teaspoons are there in a tablespoon?
- How many fluid ounces are there in one tablespoon? How many milliliters are in one tablespoon?

Fun to know

Beet Juice – an Addition to Road Salt

Beet juice is used in addition to salt to deice roads. The advantage of beet juice is that it does not cause damage to plants and animals through runoff and helps salt stay on roads longer because it is sticky. The beet juice used in deicing roads comes from food waste. So every time you have a glass of beet juice, remember it helps clear winter roads and protect the environment!

FOSSILIZED ROCKS

understanding how trace fossils are formed

Dinosaurs are mysterious and fascinating creatures. We know that they once existed because we have found their fossils. Fossils exist in many forms. Body fossils contain the remains, such as bones and leaves, of ancient animals and plants, while trace fossils do not. From fossils, we are able to find out what the lives of animals and plants were like long ago.

Small items that have details and textures, such as key chains, coins, and seashells, are great for this experiment.

What you need:

flour

salt

water

3 small items

a bowl

Difficulty: ●●●○○

Time needed:
2 days

In this experiment, you will make your own trace fossils and learn about how finding them in nature helps us know more about Earth.

What to do:

1. Pour 1 cup of flour, $\frac{1}{2}$ cup of salt, and $\frac{1}{2}$ cup of water into the bowl to make a piece of dough.
2. Divide the dough into small balls. Then flatten the balls.
3. Make the impression of each small item by pressing it hard on each piece of flattened dough.
4. Remove the small items gently and make sure the detailed impression can be seen on the dough.
5. Leave the dough pieces in a dry place overnight to let them harden to become trace fossils.
6. Ask your friends to examine the fossils. Have them guess what items left the impressions.

WHAT *just* happened?

In this experiment, you experienced the formation of trace fossils. The impressions you created on the dough left behind hints of what the items could be.

Trace fossils do not contain the body parts of animals or plants. They come in many forms: some capture the footprints of animals as they walked across ancient landscapes and some capture the trails or burrows left behind by animals as they moved or dug through the soil. These fossils preserve evidence of the creatures that once roamed Earth. Scientists study these fossils to piece together the behaviors and lifestyles of ancient animals. There are also trace fossils that include impressions of plants. These fossils show us what ancient plants looked like, giving us insights into the types of vegetation that once existed.

The study of trace fossils is exceptionally important to scientists. By examining these fossils, they can learn about the behaviors, habitats, and environments of ancient organisms.

STEM INQUIRY

- Where can fossils be found?
- What types of rocks have fossils?
- Name some dinosaurs that have been found as fossils.

- Research online with an adult's permission how fossils are preserved.

- Fossils are very fragile. How do scientists carefully remove fossils from the ground without damaging them?

- In this experiment, you made a piece of dough for making fossil impressions with the recipe provided. If you double the recipe, what amounts of the ingredients will you use? If you only use one third of the recipe, what amounts of the ingredients will you use?

Fun to know

A Record of Earth's History

Petrified Forest National Park

Petrified Forest National Park, located in Arizona, U.S., is home to one of the world's largest collections of fossilized trees dating back millions of years. It also contains ancient fossils of animals and early dinosaurs, providing a diverse record of Earth's past.

Answers

Section 1

1 Biomes

A. in gardens ; in forests
dark ; warm ; wet
leaves ; fruits

B. 1. grasses
2. elephants
3. hot
4. camels
5. water
6. treeless
7. coldest
8. precipitation
9. permafrost
10. cushion plants
11. life
12. ferns
13. insects
14. plankton
15. blue whale

C. Tropical
Location: equator
Precipitation: 60 in/1,520 mm
Temperature: warm
Animal: giant anteater, anaconda, jaguar
Plant: broad-leaved trees
Temperate
Location: equator ; Pacific
Precipitation: about 150 in/3,810 mm each year
Temperature: cool
Animal: black bear, cougar, salmon, bald eagle
Plant: giant coniferous trees

2 Habitats and Communities

A.

B.

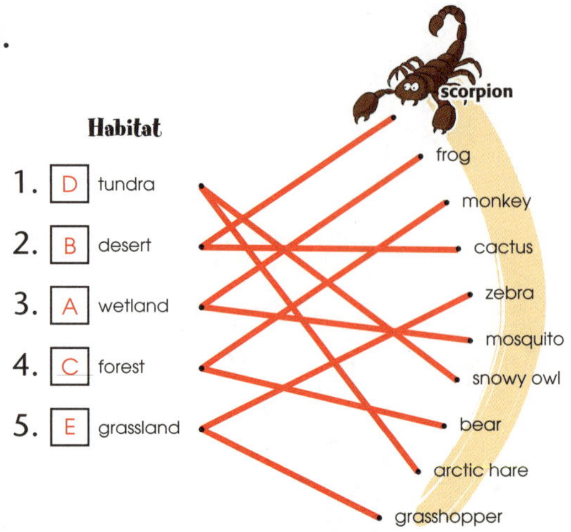

C. (Suggested features)
1. webbed feet to swim ; feathers that are waterproof
2. hard, pointed beak to crack seeds ; flexible claws to hold onto branches
3. thick stem to store water ; small spines to minimize water loss
4. thick, furry coat ; white fur to blend into the snow
5. strong, fast runner ; travel in herds to protect themselves from predators

D. 1. B
2. A
3. A ; C
4. The panda's habitat is being destroyed, so there is a huge decrease in the amount of bamboo and land space.

3 Changes to Habitats

A. A ; C ; E

B. 1. human ; deforestation
   2. natural ; wildfire
   3. human ; farming
   4. human ; oil spill
   5. natural ; flooding

C. 1. B
   2. A
   3. F
   4. C
   5. D
   6. E

D. 1. (Individual pictures)
   The Arctic:
   snow, ice, and frozen ground
   the rise of temperature
   early ice melt each spring
   Polar Bear:
   a thick layer of fat keeping them warm
   huge, rough paws giving them traction on the ice
   less food
   shrinking layer of fat for keeping warm
   2. (Suggested answer)
   Polar Bears International works to protect polar bears by funding research that educates people on the conditions of polar bears and their habitat.

4 Our Interaction with Habitats

A. (Suggested examples)
   1. jewelry
   2. cooking foil
   3. drinks
   4. jewelry
   5. electricity
   6. cooking
   7. coal ; producing heat

B. 1. A 2. C
   3. B 4. A
   5. A ; C
   (Individual idea)

C. 1. (Individual picture)
   2. It is located in Wyoming, Montana, and Idaho.
   3. Active geysers, rivers, and canyons can be found there.
   4. (Suggested answer)
   Yellowstone National Park is home to grizzly bears, wolves, pine trees, and fir trees.
   5. It is important because it allows the ecosystem to function and evolve naturally.

5 Food Chains

A. 1. A
 2. B
 3. C, D

B. 1. producers
 2. consumers
 3. decomposers
 4. Producers
 5. Consumers
 6. Decomposers

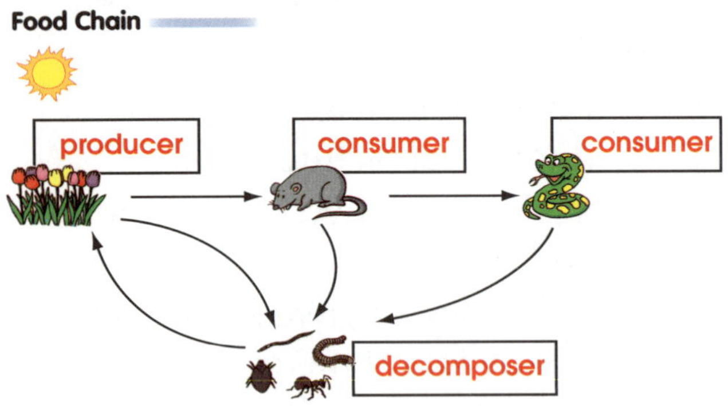

C. A: consumer
 B: producer
 C: producer
 D: decomposer
 E: consumer

D. (Suggested answers)
 1. cow
 2. grass ; fox
 3. mouse
 4. algae → shrimp → arctic cod → seal → polar bear

E. 1a. important
 b. enzymes
 c. decomposers
 d. waste
 2. Decomposers include bacteria, fungi, and worms.
 3. Decomposers break down dead plant and animal matter into essential nutrients which producers need to make food.
 4. A ; D ; E ; F

6 What Animals Eat

A. 1. C ; D ; E
   2. They have sharp teeth.
   3. They eat plants.

B. 1. Producers
   2. consumers
   3. herbivores
   4. carnivores
   5. omnivores
   6. Herbivores
   7. A: herbivore
      B: omnivore
      C: carnivore
      D: omnivore
      E: carnivore

C. 1. caterpillar
      bird (omnivore)
      bobcat (carnivore)
   2. grasshopper (herbivore)
      lizard (omnivore)
      snake (carnivore)
   3. The rest of the organisms in the food chains would die.
   4. Without the lizard eating the grasshoppers, grasshoppers would become overpopulated. This means there would not be enough grass for them to eat, and many grasshoppers would then die. Snakes would also die out because their food source was gone.

D. 1a. F
   b. T
   c. F
   d. T
   2. A blue whale's favorite food is krill. It can eat up to 40 million krill per day.
   3. plankton ; krill ; blue whale
   4. Krill would not be able to survive, and without krill, blue whales would not survive either.

Section 2

1 Machines in the Past

A. 1. inclined
easier
2. wheel ; axle
easier

B. 1. lever
2. fulcrum
3. sling
4. rock
5. rope
6. weight
7a. sling
b. rock
c. lever
d. rope
e. fulcrum
f. weight
8a. 3
b. 4
c. 2
d. 1

C. 1a. lever
b. fulcrum
c. weight
d. rope
2.

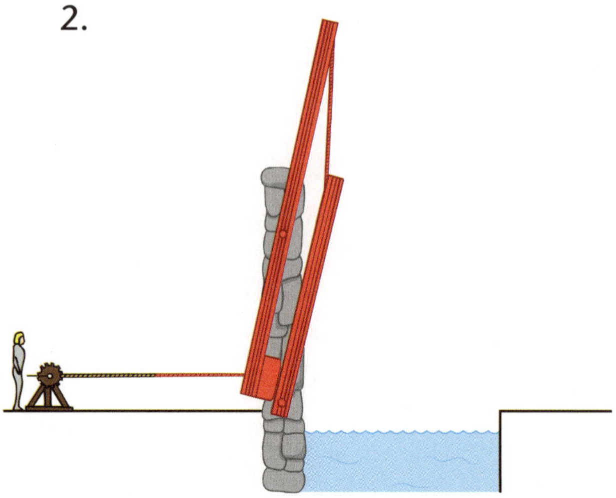

2 Simple Machines

A. A ; C ; D ; F

B. 1. A: unable
B: able
pulleys ; greater ; increased
2. counterclockwise ; faster
speeds ; small ; faster

C. 1. B
Eloise's pushing down on the stick is the effort. The small rock is the fulcrum. The large rock is the load.
2. A ; C
3. (Suggested answers)
a. pizza cutter
b. bicycle

3 Gears

A. (Make cardboard gears.)

B. 1a. counterclockwise

b. clockwise

2. yes

3.

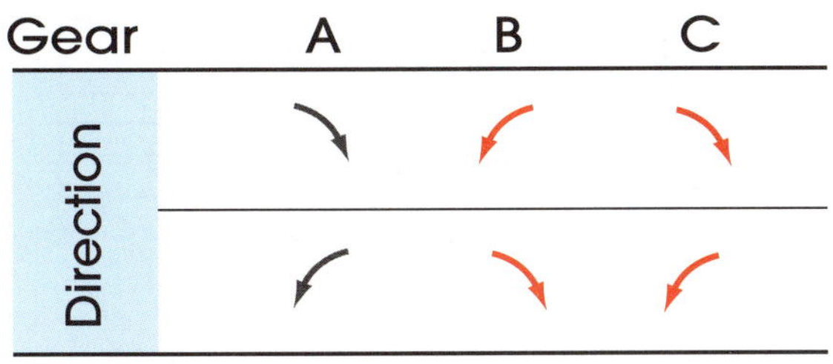

4. counterclockwise

C. 1. twice

2. faster

3. counterclockwise

4. It turns twice in a clockwise direction.

5. Yes, the speeds of both gears are the same and they move in the same direction.

D.1a. F   b. T

c. T   d. T

2. Biking on Level Ground:
front (50 teeth) and rear (15 teeth)
move fast
hard to pedal
Biking Uphill:
front (20 teeth) and rear (35 teeth)
move slowly
easy to pedal

4 Gears around Us

A. 1. lever
wheel and axle

2. screw
lever
wheel and axle

B. 1. spur gears ; shafts ; one

2. bevel gears ; direction ; two

3. worm gear ; worm ; two

4. idler gear ; same ; one

C. 1.

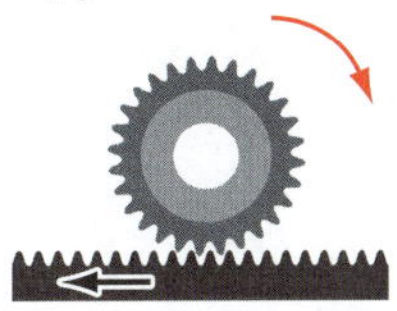
The rack moves to the left.

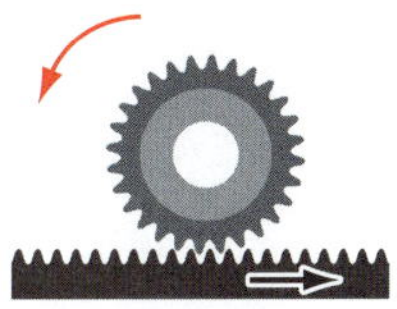
The rack moves to the right.

2. linear

3. (Suggested answers)
B ; C ; D

D.1a. no   b. yes

2. (Suggested answers)
Way 1: She can add a third gear between the dolls.

Way 2: She can move them apart and link them with a chain.

3. She can use two gears of different sizes.

5 Pulleys Everywhere

A. (Suggested answers)
A ; C ; F

B.

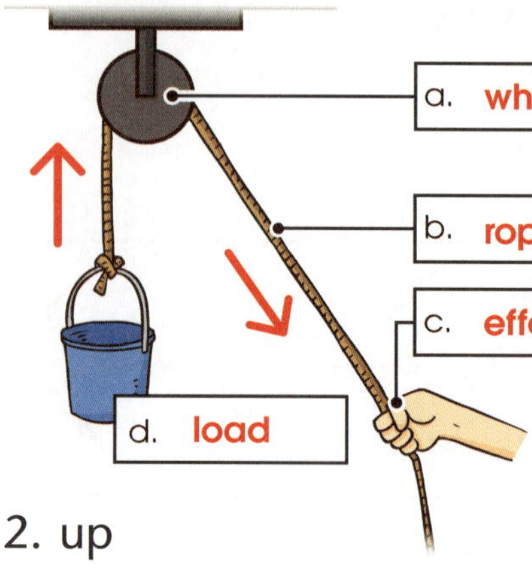

2. up

C.1a. 50 N
b. 50 N
2a. 80 N
b. 80 N
3. the same
easier
4. weight
5.

D. 1. in recreation:
pulleys – keep rock climbers safe
in construction:
cranes – move construction materials
in shipping:
forklifts – lift and lower heavy loads
in building maintenance:
pulleys – lift and lower workers on a hanging scaffolding
at home:
pulleys – lift and lower garage doors
in restaurants:
dumbwaiters – move food between floors

2a. downward
b. upward

6 Pulley Power

A. A fixed pulley at the top of the flagpole means that when you pull down on one end of the rope, the flag on the other end is raised. Your pulling is the effort.

B. 1a. 200 N
b. 100 N
2a. 420 N
b. 210 N
3. half
4. The effort needed decreases.

C. 1. Experiment 1: 100 N ; 4 in
Experiment 2: 50 N ; 8 in
2. half ; doubled
3. The distance increases.

D. 1. A
2.

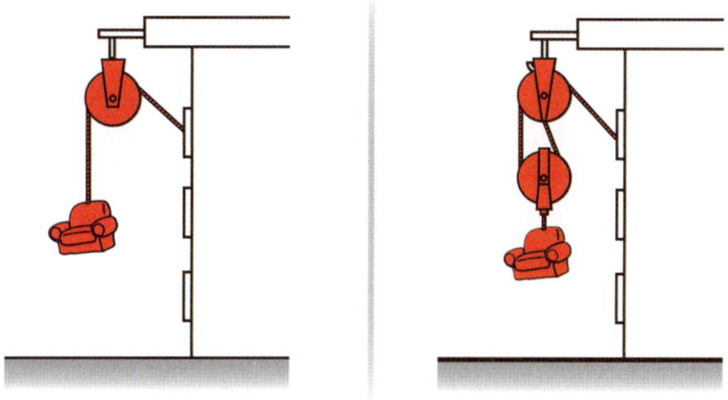

3a. 1,000 N b. 500 N

Section 3

1 Light around Us

A. (Suggested examples)
natural ; A ; sun
artificial ; B ; flashlight

B. 1. emit
2. reflect
3. emit
4. A, D, H
5. B, C, E, F, G
6. C, E, and F are safety reflectors. They keep people safe by reflecting car lights at night so that drivers can see them.

C. 1. straight
2. direction
3. reflected
4. A
5. B
6. A

2 Light: Reflection and Refraction

A.

Properties of Light

When light hits an object and bounces off, it creates a reflection.

Light travels in a straight line, but when it passes through another medium such as water, it may bend and change direction. This is called refraction.

B. 1. white
2. red
3. orange
4. yellow
5. green
6. blue
7. indigo
8. violet
9. raindrop
10. direction
11. refraction
(Color as indicated.)

C. A: white ; reflects
B: black ; absorbed
C: yellow ; absorbed
When light hits a green frog, its skin absorbs every color but green.

3 Light: Transparency

A. (Color as indicated.)
   1. transparent
   2. translucent
   3. opaque

B.

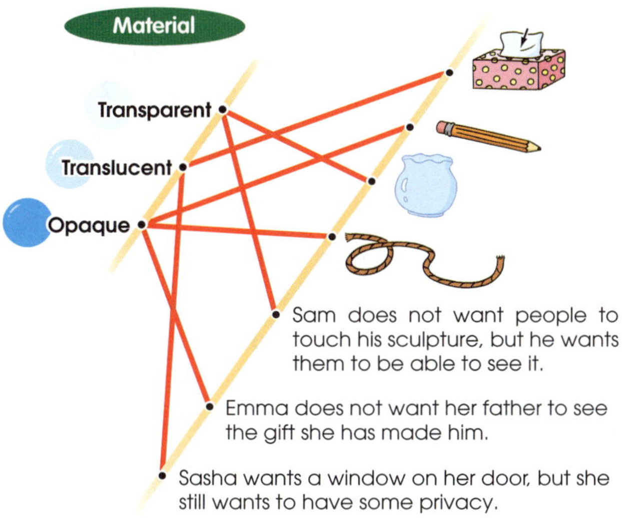

C. (Suggested answers)
   Transparent: The windshield of a car should be transparent.
   Translucent: Curtains can be translucent so that light can pass through them, but at the same time, they can provide privacy.
   Opaque: Fitting rooms for a clothing store should be opaque.

D. 1. straight
   2. shadow
   3. opaque
   4. length
   5. ✘
   6. ✔
   7. ✔

4 What Is Sound?

A. 1. vibrates
   2. vibrate
   3. vibrating
   4. sound

B. Experiment 1:
   yes ; can
   Experiment 2:
   yes ; Sound can travel through water.
   Experiment 3:
   yes ; Sound can travel through solids.

C. 1. slow ; low
   (Individual examples)
   2. fast ; high
   (Individual examples)

5 What Happens to Sound

A. 1. loudness
2. decibels
3. a jackhammer
4. a busy street
5. a whisper

B. 1. reflected ; hard
richer
An echo
2. absorbed ; soft
Carpeting
absorbing
3. modified
Loudness ; louder
Pitch ; higher

C. outer
earflap ; ear canal
eardrum
middle
tiny bones
inner
cochlea
nerves

6 How We Use Light and Sound

A.

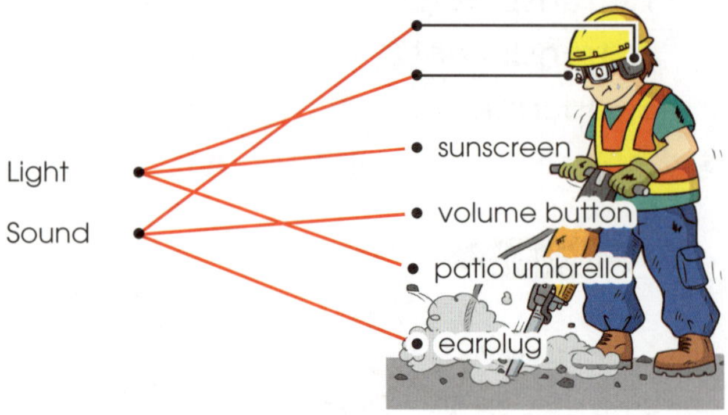

(Suggested answer)
Too much light can damage our eyes and too much sound can damage our ears.

B. 1. A ; light
2. E ; light
3. D ; light
4. B ; sound
5. C ; sound
F ; sound

C. 1. sound
2. whale
3. echolocation
4. communicate
5. echo
6. surface
7. air
8. water

Section 4

1 Rocks and Minerals

A. A ; D ; E ; F ; G ; H ; J ; K ; L
(Individual example)

B. 1. Type: mineral
inorganic
crystal
diamond
Type: rock
natural
minerals
sandstone

2. They are both solid, natural, and inorganic.

3. Minerals are made up of one thing; rocks are often made up of more than one thing.

4. rock ; mineral ; rock

C. 1. the study of Earth, including its origin, evolution, and fundamental structure.

2. rocks and minerals

3. land movement long ago

4. what is at Earth's center

5. where earthquakes are likely to happen

6. when volcanoes are likely to erupt

2 Minerals

A. 1. transparency ; translucent

2. luster ; dull

3. color

4. hardness ; soft

5. streak

B. 1. hardness

2. streak

3. luster, transparency, color

4. turquoise
waxy
opaque

5. gold
metallic
opaque

6. quartz
glassy
translucent

C. Talc
3
4
6
Quartz
9
Diamond

1. diamond

2. gypsum ; talc

3. (Suggested answer)
orthoclase and apatite

Answers

3 Rocks

A.

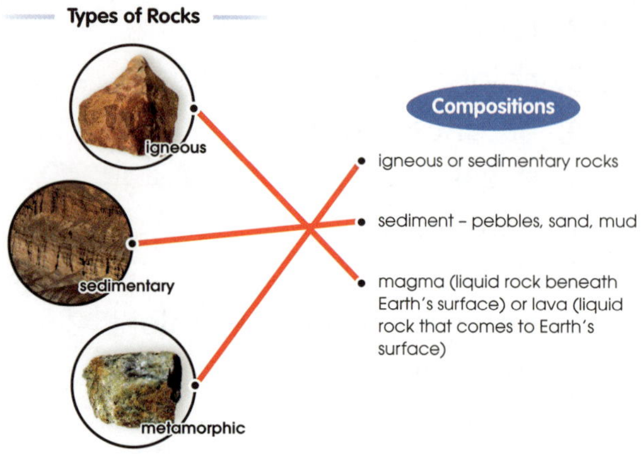

B. 1. igneous
 a. magma
  cools
  granite
 b. lava
  small
  obsidian
 2. sedimentary
  layers
  under
  fossils
  sandstone
 3. metamorphic
  extreme
  rarely
  gneiss
  marble

4 The Rock Cycle

A. 1. sand
 2. mountains
 3. moving water
 4. erosion
 5. sedimentary
 6. cycle

B. 1. sedimentary
  metamorphic
 2. igneous
  erosion
  sedimentary
 3. sedimentary
  igneous
 4. They melt into magma.
 5. They are under intense heat and pressure.
 6. They erode.
 7. They become metamorphic rocks.

C.

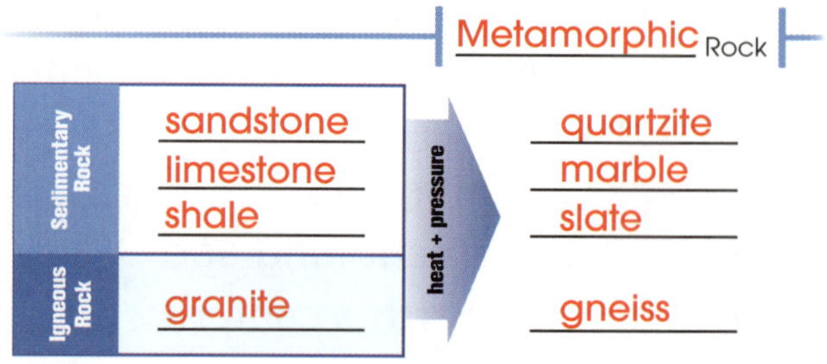

5 How We Use Rocks

A. 1. minerals
   2. ore
   3. quarries
      lead ; silver ; nickel
      gold ; tin
      iron ; aluminum

B. 1. art
      sculptures
      colors
   2. transportation
      trains
      steel
   3. construction
      concrete
   4. energy
      Coal
      Oil
   5. jewelry
      diamonds

C. 1. Rocks are important because they hold fossils, which paleontologists study.
   2. Sedimentary rocks hold fossils.
   3. 3 ; 1 ; 2

6 More about How We Use Rocks

A. Positive:
   A ; D ; E
   Negative:
   A ; B ; D ; E

B. (Suggested answers)
   1. positively ; The factory owner has raw materials to supply the factory close at hand.
   2. negatively ; The resident is worried about how the water supply will be affected.
   3. positively ; A job is guaranteed for the miner.
   4. (Suggested answer)
      Ecologist ; negatively ; The ecologist is worried about how the mine will affect the local habitat.

C. 1. aluminum
   2. melted
   3. sixty
   4. recycled
   5. mining
   6. preserve
   7. It is less expensive and it preserves resources.
   8. (Suggested answer)
      Glass is made from rocks and it can be recycled.